C000179442

K BOATS
Steam-powered submarines in World War I

Don Everitt

Airlife
England

This edition published 1999 by Airlife Publishing Ltd

First published in the UK in 1963 by George C Harrap & Co Ltd

British Library Cataloguing-in-Publication Data
  A catalogue record for this book
  is available from the British Library

ISBN 1 84037 057 2

Typeset by Phoenix Typesetting, Ilkley, West Yorkshire.

Printed in England by WBC Book Manufacturers, Bridgend, Glamorgan

Cover Painting by Lynn Williams

Airlife Publishing Ltd
101 Longden Road, Shrewsbury, SY3 9EB, England

By the same author

Samaritan of the Islands

ACKNOWLEDGEMENTS

I thank those editors, publishers and Government departments who have allowed me to quote from copyrighted material, namely:

The editor of *The Times* for the letter on p. 15, the obituary notice on p. 61 and the article on pp. 123–4;

The editor of *The Engineer* for the item on pp. 130–1;

Messrs Eyre and Spottiswoode Ltd for various small quotations from Admiral Keyes's *Naval Memoirs*;

Messrs Jonathan Cape Ltd for various small quotations from Arthur Marder's excellent trilogy of Lord Fisher's letters;

Odham's Press Ltd for the minutes on p. 11–12 taken from Churchill's *World Crisis*;

The Controller of Her Majesty's Stationery Office, for items quoted from official records and naval publications, in all of which Crown Copyright vests, and for permission to reproduce the fold-out diagram.

CONTENTS

	Introduction	9
1	Panic in the Fleet	11
2	Too Many Damned Holes	24
3	An Example of 'Bad Salvage'	39
4	K for Calamity	64
5	The Battle of May Island	76
6	The Reluctant Dip-chick	107
7	A Lethal Seesaw	117
8	. . . And Then There Were Seven	126
9	Last Fling	128
	Postscript	134
	Appendix A – The K Class	136
	Appendix B – Sources	137
	Index	141

INTRODUCTION

The most fatal error imaginable would be to put steam engines in a submarine. – Lord Fisher, former First Sea Lord, to Vice-Admiral Sir John Jellicoe, Second Sea Lord, June 1, 1913.

In the year 1915 the Admiralty laid down secretly a class of submarines of revolutionary design. These submersible destroyers, as they were called, were to be the largest, heaviest and fastest submarines built anywhere in the world at that time: indeed, they proved to be so fast that no British submarines of the 1939–45 war could have out-stripped them. They were driven on the surface by steam-engines: aft of their conning-towers they carried two retractable funnels. Between August 1916 and May 1918 the Navy commissioned seventeen of these vessels, designating them the K class.

No class of modern warship in the Royal Navy, or any other navy, has ever suffered so much calamity as the K boats. They were involved in sixteen major accidents and countless smaller mishaps. One sank on her trials. Three were lost after collisions. A fifth disappeared. Another sank in harbour. The loss of life was appalling: the escapes from death were among the most remarkable in the history of submarines.

The K boats became the objects of much superstition, hatred and contention. They were frequently described as the 'suicide club.' Many men went to extreme lengths to avoid serving in them. Yet there were others who regarded them with affection and pride.

Naval judgment on the design and purpose of the K boats has always remained sharply divided. They were intended to form a new and powerful spearhead for the Fleet, but in their two years of war service only one of them engaged the enemy, hitting a U-boat amidships with a torpedo which failed to explode. Some experts, probably the majority, have declared that the K-class submarines became obsolete before they were launched, that they were the products of bad design and bad strategy and that their continued use in the face of the many accidents typified the bigotry of many naval and military minds of that

9

era. Other experts have regarded the Ks as brilliant in conception and performance, years ahead of their time, but unhappily pursued by ill-luck.

All but one of the K disasters escaped public attention because of wartime censorship. The courts of inquiry and courts martial were held in secret. After the armistice, the Admiralty released no more information about them than the bare statistics it was obliged to give in the *Official Return of Navy Losses*. In forty years only a few brief accounts, fragmentary and often largely hearsay, have appeared in naval literature, technical journals and obituary columns. Yet in the history of the K class lies much of the chequered history of the submarine, the warship which today dominates the high seas.

A full report is overdue.

CHAPTER ONE

PANIC IN THE FLEET

I took charge of the Submarine Service in 1910 . . . For four years all our efforts were devoted to the construction of vessels capable of operating far afield on the high seas and training the personnel of ardent volunteers to fight them under war conditions. – Admiral of the Fleet Sir Roger Keyes, in 1939.

Keyes made a b- of the submarine programme. – Admiral Sir Geoffrey Layton, R.N. (Retd.), in an interview, 6 March, 1961.

In September and October of 1914 the mention of the word 'submarine' in the flagships of the Grand Fleet or in the cavernous offices of the Admiralty was likely to produce panic reaction. In Scapa Flow, the harbour in the Orkney Islands where the Fleet was thought to be safe from attack, its look-outs began to see German submarines all around. Alarms were raised several times. On 1 September, on the orders of the Commander-in-Chief, Admiral Sir John Jellicoe, the entire Fleet weighed anchor and hurried to sea, dodging and even firing on a U-boat that was never there.

The fleet laid up for seventeen days in the alternative anchorage of Loch Ewe, on the north-west coast of Scotland, then returned to the Flow. A month later, at 5 p.m. on 17 October, the same thing happened again, except that this time Loch Ewe was regarded as unsafe because a U-boat had been reported there ten days earlier. So the Grand Fleet retreated temporarily even farther from the enemy, to Lough Swilly, in Northern Ireland.

At this point, two and a half months after the start of the war with Germany, the First Lord of the Admiralty, Winston Churchill, developed a similar strained preoccupation with submarines. On 13 October he wrote to the First Sea Lord:

> Please state exactly what is the total submarine programme now sanctioned by the Cabinet or under construction in the various yards. What measures can be adopted for increasing the number of submarines? Is it possible to

let further contracts for submarines on a fifteen months' basis? It is indispensable that the whole possible plant for submarine construction should be kept at the fullest pressure night and day.

This minute clearly did not produce the result desired, for two weeks later he wrote more forcefully to the First Sea Lord:

> Please propose without delay the largest possible programme of submarine boats to be delivered in from 12 to 24 months from the present time. You should assume for this purpose that you have control of all sources of manufacture required for submarines, that there is no objection to using Vickers drawings, and that steam-engines may be used to supplement oil engines. You should exert every effort of ingenuity and organisation to secure the utmost possible delivery. As soon as your proposals are ready, which should be in the next few days, they can be considered at a conference of the Sea Lords. The Cabinet must be satisfied that the absolute maximum output is being worked to in submarines. We may be sure that Germany is doing this. Third Sea Lord's department must therefore act with the utmost vigour, and not be deterred by the kind of difficulties which hamper action in time of peace.

These minutes were remarkable. They showed a sudden and drastic change in Churchill's attitude towards submarines; and they revealed the appalling weakness of the Submarine Service.

Undoubtedly the astonishing success of the U-boats in the first weeks of the war brought about Churchill's change of mind and caused Jellicoe's jitters in Scapa Flow. On 1 September a U-boat had shocked the Grand Fleet by penetrating the Firth of Forth as far as the railway bridge. Four days later another U-boat had torpedoed the flotilla-leader *Pathfinder* in the Channel. Then on 22 September, the submarine U9 had sunk the British cruisers *Aboukir, Hogue* and *Cressy,* the latter being torpedoed as they stopped to rescue men from the *Aboukir.* Out of crews totalling more than 2,200 men, 1,459 died that morning.

This catastrophe led to an order stopping all movements of Allied ships in the Channel by daylight and forbidding troop transports to leave for France except from West Country ports. By 15 October when U9 scored another success, sinking the cruiser *Hawke* and killing five hundred men, the top British naval minds became unbalanced about submarines. It was a condition which had an unhappy influence on the Submarine Service for a long time to come.

Of sixty-four submarines in commission in the Royal Navy at the outbreak of the war, only seventeen could operate beyond the coasts of Britain. The remainder were from six to ten years old, and obsolete.

Germany had concentrated in the past two years on the development of Oversea U-boats with a reported range of 3,000 miles, and she was known to have twenty-eight in Service on 4 August. Rumours put the figure much higher. Lord 'Jacky' Fisher, the former First Sea Lord, had heard from a reliable Danish source that Germany had forty-six Oversea U-boats. After the sinking of the four British cruisers the Naval Intelligence Division itself gave credence to an unlikely report that the enemy had built secretly '100 to 200 small submarines'. Certainly Germany had announced before the war a programme for building seventy-two U-boats, and her shipyards, unlike their British counterparts, were filled with foreign orders for submarines, which were easily appropriated in time of war.

The explanation for the material weakness of the Submarine Service in October 1914 lay in its mismanagement before the war. That there had been mismanagement was undisputed. But exactly when it had occurred and who was responsible were the subjects of heated argument.

Lord Fisher, who was recalled as First Sea Lord on 30 October, and was therefore faced immediately with implementing the orders in Churchill's minutes, openly blamed Commodore Roger Keyes, then Flag Officer (Submarines), for 'making a d___d mess of the submarines'. A decade before, Fisher, in his first period as First Sea Lord, had laid the foundations of the Submarine Service in the face of tremendous opposition. Politicians and naval officers called him a lunatic and his submarines playthings. He had to 'hide the money for them in the Estimates'. But Fisher saw the submarine as 'the coming dreadnought'. As early as 1904 he said, 'I don't think it is even faintly realised – the immense impending revolution which the submarines will effect as offensive weapons of war.' At the same time other senior officers were calling them 'the weapons of the weaker nations' and 'underhand, unfair and damned un-English'. Even the Navy's first Inspecting Captain of Submarines, Captain Edgar Lees, said, 'The British Navy has never wanted submarine boats, but a share in their evolution has been of late forced upon us by other nations.'

When Churchill recalled Fisher as First Sea Lord in October 1914 the admiral was appalled to find that the Navy had twelve fewer submarines than it had on his retirement in January 1910. 'There never was such a mistake', he wrote, 'as putting Keyes in charge of the submarines.' He had not the 'faintest idea of how to employ them'. And, 'sadder still,' there had not been the 'slightest improvement in our submarines in four years'. Fisher blamed other high-ranking officers for this fiasco, but never Winston Churchill, the man who had held the supreme responsibility for all naval building during the four years in question. The naval estimates which the First Lord put through Parliament in 1912, 1913 and 1914 were the costliest ever up to that date, but little of the money went to the Submarine Service. It was not that the First Lord was unaware of the growing numbers of German submarines. In February of 1912 he told the Cabinet that in Germany's estimates for submarines that year there was 'an increase on the already large provision of £750,000'. Fisher, though in retirement at this time, remained Churchill's valued, unofficial counsellor; but the one piece of advice that Churchill consistently ignored was to build more submarines. In January of 1914 Fisher told him 'for the twentieth time since he became First Lord that the weak point of his administration is the neglect of submarines'. Normally explosively outspoken, the admiral seemed strangely reluctant to get into an argument with Churchill. In a letter to Admiral Jellicoe on 1 June, 1913, he said:

> Krupp's, the German arms firm, were making hundreds of submarine engines of a far larger power than ours . . . I am extremely anxious about the Admiralty development of the submarine. The more I hear, the more d____d fools they seem to be! I've written a memorandum on the subject, but if I sent it to Winston it would mean open war with the Admiralty so I withhold it . . .

Later, Fisher 'let fly' at the Prime Minister, Asquith, about the submarine shortage. 'He is evidently greatly moved,' Fisher wrote afterwards, 'but he entreated me to say nothing!'

In common with most members of the Cabinet and most senior naval officers, Churchill held that the submarine, as yet slow, comparatively unseaworthy and unable to keep pace with the Fleet, could serve only as a coastal defence weapon. Yet Fisher was not the only man with foresight. It was not a case of Churchill's ignoring one particular bee in his trusted adviser's bonnet. In the winter of 1913–14 a writer in the newly published *Naval Review*, which was circulated privately and confidentially to naval officers, condemned 'the present ostrich policy of ignoring the effects that the submarine should now have upon our naval policy'. He argued that because Britain was not building enough submarines she had theoretically lost command of the North Sea, the Channel, and the Mediterranean. The submarine, he said, was not governed by the accepted laws of strategy and tactics: in considering its behaviour and effects, the teachings of history were valueless.

But the Admiralty hierarchy did not agree. When Fisher forecast in 1912 and again in January 1914 that in the next war enemy submarines would sink unarmed British merchantmen without warning, Churchill did not believe that 'this would be done by a civilised Power'. He was equally unconvinced when, on 5 June, 1914, Admiral Sir Percy Scott, the gunnery expert and friend of Fisher, wrote to *The Times*:

> Submarines and aeroplanes have entirely revolutionised naval warfare; no fleet can hide itself from the aeroplane eye, and the submarine can deliver a deadly attack even in broad daylight . . .Under these circumstances, I can see no use for battleships, and very little chance of much employment for fast cruisers.

The excessive far-sightedness of Scott's letter achieved the opposite reaction from the one he sought. He aimed to awaken the Government, the First Lord, the Admiralty and the public to the new danger. Instead, they scoffed. But three months later, in broad daylight, U9 sank *Aboukir, Hogue* and *Cressy*.

Commodore Keyes, whose term as Flag Officer (Submarines) practically coincided with Churchill's at the Admiralty, had nothing but praise for the First Lord. Keyes, a man of great daring, charm and ambition, wrote that before Churchill took office it was:

> extraordinarily difficult to make progress towards the provision of a large force of submarines . . . in the face of the ponderous machinery of a departmental Admiralty, and the doubts of many senior naval officers as to the value of submarines in war. And then came Winston Churchill and the whole atmosphere changed . . . He was keenly interested, and from that moment the Submarine Service had a warm friend and supporter.

From this it might reasonably be supposed that progress was made towards 'the provision of a large force of submarines' and that Churchill was the fairy godfather of the Submarine Service. But this is a supposition not borne out by the facts.

Keyes reckoned that the Service was in a bad shape when he took over; and he had no doubt about who was to blame: it was Fisher. He accused the Admiral of giving Messrs Vickers, Sons and Maxim, of Barrow-in-Furness, a monopoly of submarine-building in Britain. Since 1904, it was true, Vickers had held exclusive rights to the patents of the American naval architect John P. Holland, whose designs were used extensively in the first British submarines. Keyes protested that this arrangement, which required two years' notice of termination,

15

forced him to look abroad for new designs. Accordingly there were
visits to the dockyards at Spezia and Toulon. They resulted in orders
for three submarines of Italian design being placed with Messrs Scott,
of Greenock, and for four of French design with Messrs Armstrong
Whitworth.

But Keyes could hardly claim that the foreign excursions had saved
time: the Armstrong Whitworth order was not placed until 1913, when
the Vickers arrangement had been ended anyway. What does seem
remarkable is that during the previous two years, while French,
German, Danish and Italian yards were busy producing submarines
to their own designs, Britain could not build one original submarine.

Keyes rounded on Vickers, too. He said the firm:

> had been given orders for Oversea submarines to their full building
> capacity, but they had entirely failed to keep pace with our requirements,
> with the result that we had fallen behind Germany, who had avoided our
> mistake and built nothing but Oversea submarines for some years.

This statement was not borne out by a letter written by Fisher on
25 May, 1914: 'The story is that Vickers will soon be discharging submarine workmen for want of orders (you can verify this by asking
Trevor Dawson!).' Sir Trevor Dawson was managing director of
Vickers.

Keyes also attacked Fisher for causing the shortage of Oversea
submarines in 1914 by concentrating on the production of small
coastal submarines in the years up to 1910. Keyes should not have
made so feeble an excuse because, after the visits to the Continental
yards, he himself had ordered submarines of no greater range, size or
armament than those which Fisher had laid down before his retirement. He dissipated the submarine strength on a motley collection of
foreign designs and modifications of those designs, disregarding warn-
ings that it would be difficult, if not impossible, to get the machinery
to finish the submarines if war broke out. It was for precisely this
reason that the production of several of the submarines was delayed
for months.

By 1913 Keyes had at last called upon Vickers and Scott to produce
an original Oversea design. Vickers presented drawings for a submarine twice the size of the largest class then in service, and with a range
of 5,300 miles. The Scott design was much smaller, and was accompanied by a surprising proposal. The firm was not prepared to
guarantee the reliability of the Italian Fiat engines, which it built under
licence, and it suggested using steam turbines instead. Keyes seized
upon this idea. 'We viewed with misgivings the much more powerful

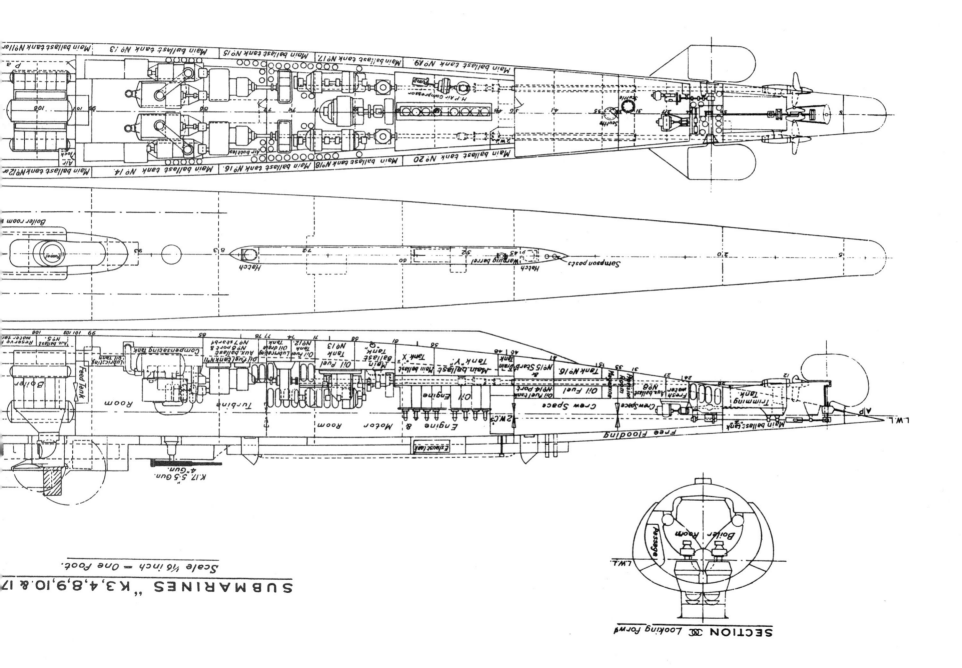

SUBMARINES "K3,4,8,9,10.& 17"

Scale 1/16 inch = One Foot.

SECTION XX Looking forward

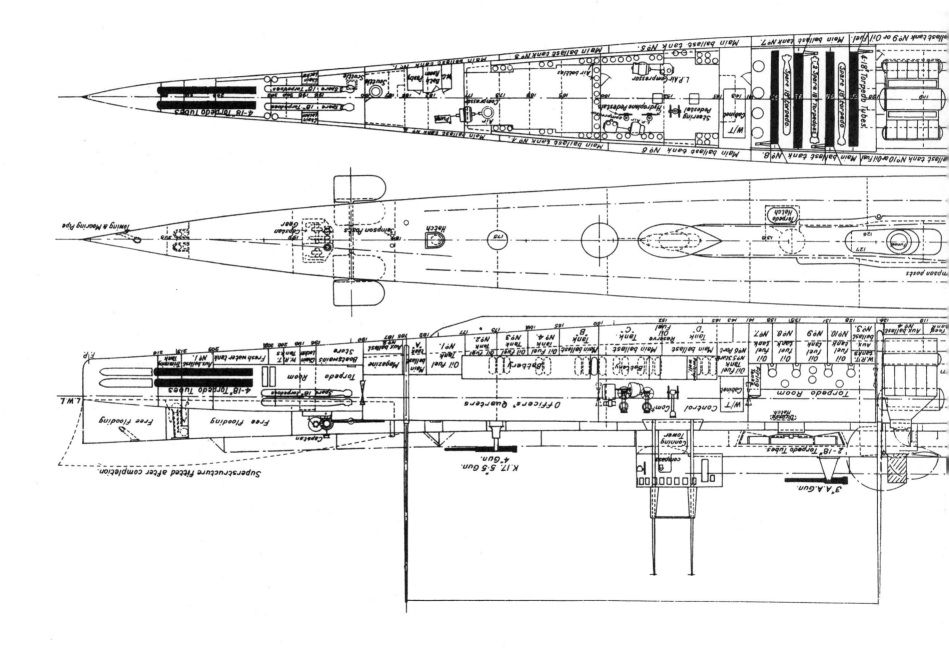

engines necessary to propel Vickers' Oversea ... We welcomed, therefore, with relief the introduction of such a simple and well-tried means
of propulsion as a steam turbine.' Keyes ordered one each of both
designs. The Vickers boat was named *Nautilus,* the other *Swordfish.*
What the Admiralty later called 'the novelty' of steam-engines in the
Swordfish was kept strictly secret.

Many naval officers, particularly submarine commanders, were
openly sceptical about the use of steam-engines and funnels in
submarines. Lord Fisher had plenty to say. In June of 1913 he wrote:

> The oil engine will govern all sea-fighting, and all sea-fighting is going to be
> governed by submarines, and yet like d___ d fools we are only spending as
> much money on them as the Germans and we are behind them in the oil
> engine, and so like the French we are fatally hankering after steam engines
> in submarines.

In the spring of 1913 the Director of Naval Construction, Sir Eustace
Tennyson-d'Eyncourt, produced another design for a steam-driven
submarine, described by Keyes as an Ocean type. It was a prodigious
size, 338 feet long and displacing some 1,700 tons. This was twice the
length and three times the displacement of the E-class submarines, the
largest then in commission. It was bigger than many destroyers. The
proposed engines would give a surface speed of 24 knots, nine knots
faster than the E class, and its armament was to consist of four 21-inch
bow torpedo tubes, four similar beam tubes and two guns. It would
have a range of 3,000 miles. A model of it was tested in the tank at
Haslar Creek, Portsmouth, but a conference called by the Third Sea
Lord soon afterwards decided 'not to proceed further with the design'.
The objections raised at the conference, which was attended by Keyes
and d'Eyncourt, were:

a. The great increase in size over boats in commission.
b. The use of steam for surface propulsion.
c. The problems of control involved when diving and when
submerged.

From the time of that conference up to October of 1914 nothing
developed to influence the objections. Indeed, in Scott's yard at
Greenock the *Swordfish* presented its builders with seemingly endless
problems and after fourteen months' work was not half finished.

Against this background, Churchill's authorisation in his minute of
28 October, 1914, that 'steam engines may be used to supplement oil
engines' was clearly made in desperation. But it was because of the

broader background of bungling that he had to resort to desperate retrogressive steps to build a submarine fleet.

To his credit, Fisher, resuming office at seventy-three as First Sea Lord, did not allow the panic over the submarine shortage to affect his judgment. He flung himself with his customary fanatical energy into the task Churchill had set him. Within forty-eight hours of taking office on 30 October, he called a meeting of the senior submarine officers and the appropriate Admiralty officials; and he began the proceedings by telling the Superintendent of Contracts that he would make his wife a widow and his house a dunghill if he brought paper-work or red tape into the business. 'I want submarines, not contracts', he said. A week later representatives of ship-building firms from all over Britain attended a conference at the Admiralty. By the end of the day Fisher placed orders with twelve firms for thirty-eight submarines. A few days later he ordered six more from British yards and ten from the Bethlehem Steel Corporation of America. He had a medley of designs to choose from as a result of Keyes's pre-war efforts: sixteen submarines of six different experimental types were at that moment being built up and down the country. Fisher ignored them all, scorned Churchill's suggestion of using steam-engines and ordered from the British yards only modified versions of the proven E class which he himself had laid down five years before. The American design, known as the H class, was equally well tried. The final testimony to Fisher's judgment lay in the magnificent war record of the E class and its derivative, the G class. Keyes's experimental boats on the other hand, achieved little. The S and W classes, being unsuited to northern waters, were sold to Italy when she entered the war, and the V and F classes were discarded.

No sooner had Fisher's War Emergency Programme of November 1914 relieved fears about the submarine shortage than another scare began. Flag officers afloat reported that German submarines had much higher surface speeds than British submarines. One was said to have travelled at 22 knots. The loss of the battleship *Formidable*, torpedoed by a U-boat early on New Year's Day, 1915, aggravated the rumour. In a gale the U-boat was said to have kept pace with the battleship, from which 547 of the crew of 780 were lost. Fisher himself was taken in by the stories, which were based on doubtful observations at sea. He wrote to Jellicoe, on 4 January, 1915: 'We can't touch their submarines. We know that two of them have gone 19 knots on the surface . . .'

He ordered the Director of Naval Construction to design immediately a submarine capable of at least 20 knots on the surface.

Thereupon d'Eyncourt once more proposed the use of steam turbines, pointing out that no diesel submarine yet designed for the Navy had exceeded 15½ knots. To produce another four and a half knots from existing engines was asking too much. With steam, d'Eyncourt said, he could guarantee more than 20 knots.

Two months earlier instinct and common sense had told Fisher that boilers, funnels and submarines did not mix. Since then the experiences of a small, steam-driven French submarine, *Archimède*, had vindicated his decision. *Archimède* had been attached temporarily to Roger Keyes's command. On 17 December she was stationed with seven British submarines in a line across the Heligoland Bight, ready to trap Admiral Hipper's battle-cruiser squadron on its return from bombarding Scarborough and Hartlepool. That evening a heavy sea struck and so bent *Archimède's* funnel that it could not be lowered sufficiently to close the watertight hatch for diving. The weather worsened, and water poured down the buckled funnel. The crew, which included a British liaison officer, Lieutenant-Commander Godfrey Herbert, formed a bucket chain to bale out the boiler-room. At dawn the submarine lay on the surface, unable to submerge. She was almost within sight of Heligoland, an easy target for any passing patrol boat. For two days she crawled westward. The storm, which kept the baling parties working continuously, fortunately confined the enemy's patrols to harbour, and *Archimède* puffed her way safely to Harwich. Fisher heard of this incident later when he received the report of the submarines' failure to engage the German battle-cruisers. He quoted it in telling d'Eyncourt that he wanted to hear no more about steam-engines.

Accordingly, by the end of January 1915, the construction department designed a diesel submarine which, d'Eyncourt said, would achieve 21 knots. Its motive-power consisted of three engines of the type used in the E-class submarines. There were no fewer than 36 cylinders. On 29 January Fisher authorised the construction of eight of these submarines, designated the J class, at the dockyards at Portsmouth, Devonport and Pembroke.

This counter-measure against the allegedly fast German submarines appeased the flag officers of the Grand Fleet, but only temporarily. The real trouble was that most senior naval officers had an obsession about the ideal rôle for submarines in war. They believed that battle fleets should have their own flotillas of submarines, capable of working with the surface ships at their routine speed of 21 knots. This obsession was not shared by most practising submarine officers and ratings, who did not relish the prospect of submerging and manoeuvring literally within striking distance of the keels of their own battle fleet. It seems remarkable now that anyone ever regarded the submarine as other than a lone, unsupported weapon. The explanation for the flag officers' obsession lay in their rigid faith in traditional naval strategy. They believed that the Navy's prime function in the war would be to engage in fleet actions, battles staged between opposing armadas. To lead a victorious fleet in the Nelson manner had been the dream of most midshipmen since Trafalgar. It was no less the dream of Jellicoe, Sir David Beatty and other flag officers in 1914. Their waking hours were dedicated to planning and rehearsing fleet battles. Churchill, too, was certain that the German Navy 'was intended for a great trial of strength with the navy of the greatest Naval Power'. If submarines could be built to accompany the Fleet, British admirals could use them as surprise weapons to hit the enemy fleet as it deployed or retreated.

Commodore Keyes, who had charge of the submarines for four years, but never served in them, shared this dream of operating them with the Grand Fleet. In 1913 he had tried the plan in an exercise between opposing fleets. It was a portentous experience. Four submarines, a mile apart and in line abreast, joined one of the fleets behind the forward screen of cruisers. The idea was that the cruisers should notify Keyes, in the destroyer *Swift*, of the movements of the opposition fleet, and he would direct his submarines to dive and attack at the appropriate moment. All this was played out in slow time because the fleet accompanying the submarines could go no faster than the submarines' top speed of 14 knots, a factor which, as Keyes conceded, made the exercise 'a somewhat primitive effort'. He confessed to having:

> some very bad moments . . . watching heavy ships, cruisers and destroyers manoeuvring in all directions over the submarines, and for some hours I was in mortal fear that one of the submarines had come to grief; however, she rose at last and all was well.

After all this, and in spite of the speed restrictions, he called the exercise successful.

In the first month of the war, Keyes's submarines had put their peace-time experience to the test, and gone into action with the surface ships in the Heligoland Bight. The results were near-disastrous. Submarine captains three times mistook the British ships for the enemy. A torpedo from E6 narrowly missed the cruiser *Lowestoft*. Three British cruisers in turn mistook the British submarines for U-boats and tried to ram them. Still no lessons were learned. 'The submarines had proved', said Keyes, 'that they could be trusted to work in co-operation with surface craft and take care of themselves.'

Even Fisher believed in fleet submarines. 'Without any doubt,' he said, 'a fast Battle Fleet which can be accompanied always by submarines under all circumstances would possess an overwhelming fighting advantage.' It was one of the few subjects about which he and Keyes agreed. When Fisher laid down the eight J-class boats in January 1915 he intended to use them as fleet submarines.

Two weeks later the friction between him and Keyes reached a climax. Keyes was sent to the Dardanelles, then in 1918 won lasting fame as the leader of the naval force which scuttled block-ships in the mouth of the Zeebrugge harbour. Years later, recalling his submarine command, he wrote: 'I do not think that *matériel* is much in my line.'

In Keyes's place Lord Fisher appointed Commodore Sydney Hall, who had previously commanded the Submarine Service from 1906 to 1910. Hall believed in fleet submarines, too.

Two months after his appointment Hall had to tell Fisher that it now appeared that the J class would not exceed 19 knots, two knots too slow for fleet work. Jellicoe, Beatty, Hall and others whose judgment Fisher trusted repeatedly impressed on him that the provision of fleet submarines with a guaranteed speed of 21 knots was vitally urgent. They felt that Germany, with her superiority in diesel engine design, would soon equip herself with fleet submarines, if she had not already done so. To counter the menace the Grand Fleet must equip itself similarly, no matter what the cost. Then Messrs Vickers weighed in with a report that they could extract no more power or speed from their existing designs of diesel engines, and they proposed and submitted drawings for a steam-driven submarine.

Under this pressure Fisher's resistance to steam began to crack. D'Eyncourt's 1913 design was brought out yet again, and compared with the Vickers design. His was obviously the better, being one knot faster at 24 knots, but certain of the Vickers ideas were worth using. The arguments in favour of steam were pressed forward. Here was a submarine guaranteed to work with the Fleet. The matter was critical. The Fleet was being deprived of a vital arm. Sir Eustace's design was infinitely superior to the French *Archimède*. The system of closing the funnels and vents was demonstrably foolproof. Would the First Sea Lord not reconsider his decision?

Fisher gave in.

At his suggestion an auxiliary diesel engine was incorporated in the design as a safety device, and to shorten the excessive time required to dive and get under way after surfacing. This gave the new submarine seven power units: two steam turbines for surface propulsion, four electric motors for submerged propulsion and the diesel motor.

Another modification concerned the boiler-room, which would become so hot immediately after a dive that no one could survive in it. In d'Eyncourt's original design the boiler-room was merely sealed off, so that the men in the engine-room and crew's quarters were cut off from those in the forward compartments. Now a communicating passage was to be installed alongside the boiler-room. A third amendment to the 1913 design gave the submarine three guns, not two, and replaced the eight 21-inch torpedo tubes with ten 18-inch tubes, because these were already in production. The two additional tubes were to be fitted in the funnel superstructure for use on the surface at night.

Fisher sanctioned four of the new submarines. On 4 May, 1915, d'Eyncourt sent his drawings to Vickers, requesting the earliest delivery dates and the terms for two of them. 'It is specially desired', he said, 'that every possible precaution may be taken to ensure the absolute secrecy of this proposal and of the nature of the work whilst under construction.' On 18 June the Admiralty contracts department accepted Vickers's proposition of about £300,000 per boat, and work began. At the same time the other two boats were ordered from Portsmouth dockyard.

Thus the K class was born.

On 17 May, 1915, Lord Fisher resigned as First Sea Lord in protest over the Dardanelles campaign and, as he put it, 'because of absolute incompatibility of view with the First Lord'. Ten more K boats were ordered as soon as he had gone, three of them from Vickers, three from naval dockyards, two from the Tyne yard of Armstrong Whitworth and two from the Fairfield yard on the Clyde.

Between September of that year and May of 1916 a six-man Submarine Development Committee met several times at the Admiralty to consider the Navy's needs. With the first K boats still on the stocks and untried, d'Eyncourt hankered after bigger and faster steam submarines. He proposed a cruiser submarine capable of 30 knots. In successfully advising the committee to turn it down, Commodore Hall admitted that he had begun to have reservations about the K class. He was hearing almost daily that the experimental, steam-driven *Swordfish*, which had at last been completed, was giving nothing but trouble to her captain, Commander Geoffrey Layton. Condensation in the engine-room after diving was short-circuiting the main switchboard, and at least one member of the crew had suffered a severe burn. In the cramped boiler-room a flashback had burned another man's face. Worst of all, the submarine showed a tendency to roll over when trimmed down for diving. When he heard about d'Eyncourt's proposals Hall wrote to the Third Sea Lord:

> It [the K class] must be considered a very bold advance in submarine design, being an increase of over 300 per cent on anything previously tried . . . It is not yet certain that high speed will always carry tactical advantage . . . Generally speaking, in submarines the power to submerge takes the place of high speed . . . a high-speed submarine will have many disadvantages. Her length makes her a great target for torpedo attack. Her visibility makes her easier to stalk by hostile submarines. It is true that high speed enables her to zigzag and renders her more difficult to hit, but the balance is considered to leave her with disadvantage. Underwater she is made unhandy to manoeuvre quickly for torpedo attack, and she requires deep water to work in. She is more likely to strike mines, on the surface and submerged. She is also more costly and a much greater anxiety to the personnel . . . Only the necessity of accompanying the battle fleet justified in my opinion the size of the K class . . .

In any event, it was too late now for second thoughts.

CHAPTER TWO

TOO MANY DAMNED HOLES

Special arrangements had to be made for shutting down watertight the funnels, etcetera. However, all these difficulties were overcome and the boats were very successful. – Sir Eustace Tennyson-d'Eyncourt to the Institute of Naval Architects, 9 April, 1919.

When Lieutenant-Commander Godfrey Herbert and his wife Elizabeth awoke early in the morning of 29 January, 1917, they regarded the day as one which would be significant in their lives, though for different reasons. For Herbert, the day would end, if all went well, with his signing the acceptance forms, on behalf of His Britannic Majesty, for the new submarine, K13. He would have command of a vessel again, and tomorrow his orders would arrive to join the Fleet. The past three and a half months had made an enjoyable break, but he was a practical man who felt that in war the only thing to do was to fight. For his wife, the day would end an unexpected period of domesticity. They had married in London the previous May and Herbert had returned immediately to sea. Then in October had come the posting to stand by the submarine building at Govan, on the Clyde, and they had taken lodgings in Glasgow. Today, for Elizabeth Herbert, life would become insecure again.

Her husband left the house at 6.30 a.m. saying he would be back for dinner. Outside the air was still but searchingly cold. Herbert, thirty-two years old, a mettlesome, stalwart Warwickshire man with a formidable jutting jaw, strode briskly through the grey streets. From the clear sky conditions looked ideal for the acceptance trials. At Fairfield's yard he joined the stream of men who filed singly or in pairs to the basin where K13 lay alongside. At that time on a cold morning they had little to say to one another beyond acknowledgements. Herbert, having inspected the submarine the previous day, cast a brief glance over the upper deck, then joined the others stepping down the conning-tower into the brightness, the warmth and the bustle of the control-room. Men crowded the submarine, making final checks of machinery. Herbert ran through the day's arrangements with his first lieutenant, Lieutenant Paris Graham Singer. A grandson of the American inventor of the sewing-machine, Singer was twenty-four, tall and angular, with dark brooding features and an intense manner.

At eight o'clock, exactly on schedule, everything was ready. Eighty men were on board: the crew of fifty-three, who were to operate the submarine (though it remained the property of the Fairfield Shipbuilding Company till Herbert signed the acceptance forms); fourteen directors and employees of Fairfield's; five representatives of sub-contracts; five Admiralty officials; a Clyde pilot; and two passengers, the commanding and engineer officers of K14, which was being built at the same yard. On top of the conning-tower, from behind a waist-high canvas screen which was intended to afford protection from the sea and the elements, Herbert gave the order to cast off and tugs towed the giant submarine out of the basin. Her twin funnels belching diesel smoke, she moved slowly down the Clyde.

Things went wrong from the start. Not a mile from the Fairfield berth, opposite the district of Whiteinch, someone accidentally switched off the starter motor on the steering-gear, putting the helm out of action. Before there was time to hold her with the engines, her bows swung gently towards the port side of the river and grounded on a mud-bank. The ebbing tide at once began to pull her stern downstream. She pivoted on her bows, spreading her great length across the river. At the same time a Glasgow steamer called *Sonnava* was heading up-river towards her. Herbert warned her to keep clear with a series of Ds in Morse code on the submarine's siren. But the steamer came on, trying to pass through the gap between the stern of K13 and a dredger, the *Shieldhall*, which lay alongside a quay on the other side of the river. The gap was too narrow. With a screeching of metal, the *Sonnava* sandwiched herself between the submarine and the dredger. Colourful expletives rose from the bridges of both vessels. The tide was ebbing swiftly, and the situation was likely to become grossly embarrassing, to say the least, if the vessels were not cleared quickly. The port authorities would not be amused to have a submarine lying athwart the river for six hours till the next high tide.

The *Sonnava* thrashed astern and freed herself. Herbert allowed the tide to carry the submarine about until she was heading stern first down the river, then ordered full astern on both engines. She slid grudgingly off the mud, and proceeded, somewhat ingloriously, stern first down the Clyde until, at a tributary known as the Cart, Herbert had room to put her about.

By eleven o'clock she reached Craigendoran Pier and took on board Hugh Macmillan, a Fairfield director, and Professor Percy Hillhouse,

25

the firm's naval architect. By eleven-thirty she was off the Tail of the Bank, on the broad sheet of the estuary off Greenock, and her steam turbines were worked up to full power. Herbert put her through the routine procedures of a surface trial: starting, speed variations, stopping, turning, going astern. All went smoothly. At noon he headed her for her final diving trials into the comparative seclusion of the Gareloch, the finger of water seven miles long with points into the hills on the north side of the Clyde. The day was fine and balmy now, and the submarine swept through placid water. At the head of the loch a small steamer called *Comet*, which was acting as tender to K13, took on board for lunch those men whose services were not needed for the dive. Herbert ordered the rest of the crew to diving stations, and trimmed her down till the base of the conning tower was level with the surface of the loch. 'Dive eight feet', he ordered. A mile and a half down the loch, opposite the sprawling Shandon Hydropathic Hotel, he brought her to the surface. During the submerged run she had steadily increased her depth. Herbert suggested to the Fairfield men that she had gained weight. Just then his engineer officer, Engineer-Lieutenant Arthur Lane, came from aft to say that the boiler-room had sprung a small leak, and about 200 gallons of water had collected. The heat and steam in the boiler-room during the dive had prevented Lane from trying to find the source of the leak, so he proposed that they should submerge again after lunch. Herbert agreed. He gave orders for the boiler-room to be pumped dry and thoroughly ventilated in the meantime.

Before boarding the *Comet* for lunch Lane asked the Admiralty overseer, Frederick Searle, to look at one of the boiler-room ventilators with him. There were four ventilators in all, each 37 inches in diameter, clustered between the funnels. They were closed for diving by mushroom-type hatches which lowered on to rubber seatings. Lane told Searle that the hatch on the port after-ventilator was sticking. He showed him that it was not fully open by three-quarters of an inch. The overseer assured him that there was nothing to worry about. The engineer's caution was understandable. This was his first appointment to a submarine. Indeed, previous classes had not required engineer officers. The son of an engineer rear-admiral, he had a reputation for reliable, painstaking work and sound judgment. These qualities had marked him out for his present job.

On board the *Comet* Herbert told the Fairfield directors that he was generally satisfied with the boat, and would accept her on condition that she went into dry dock back at the yard for an inspection for damage caused by the grounding up the river.

Had he been superstitious, as submariners often are, Herbert might have regarded the mishaps so far that day as unhappy omens, particularly on a vessel numbered 13. But he had an even, uncomplicated temperament, which helped to explain why, even though submarines had several times almost cost him his life, he preferred to serve in them. Ten years earlier, for example, when he had been first lieutenant of A4, she had sunk in the Solent during an early experiment in underwater signalling. She had been lying submerged with a brass tubular ventilator, four inches in diameter, projecting slightly above the surface. It was intended that a torpedo boat should cruise at increasing distances from A4, periodically ringing a bell. So long as the captain of A4, Lieutenant Martin Naismith, could hear the bell through a megaphone attached to the submarine's hull he would wave a red flag on the end of a boathook passed through the ventilator tube. The ill-devised experiment never got going. The wash of a passing steamer swept over the ventilator, and water gushed into the submarine, immediately affecting her trim. Forty degrees down by the bows, she plunged ninety feet to the sea-bed. The incoming salt water reached the batteries, which threw off dense and lethal chlorine fumes. While the other men stuffed caps and a jersey into the open tube to try to stem the leak, Herbert, groping in the darkness, blew the ballast tanks. After three and a half minutes A4 shot to the surface, and her choking crew clambered up to the conning-tower to safety.

Another time, in November 1914, Herbert had a narrower escape when the submarine he was commanding, D5, struck a mine off Harwich. A few minutes earlier he had taken over on the conning-tower from his first lieutenant. A Gorleston drifter picked him up with four members of his crew after they had been swimming almost fully clothed for more than half an hour. Nineteen men, including the first lieutenant, were lost. A month later Herbert sailed as liaison officer in the ill-starred French steam submarine, *Archimède*, which bent its funnel in high seas in the Heligoland Bight and barely managed to crawl back to Harwich.

In 1915, in a respite from submarine duties, he had commanded one of the first secretly armed merchantmen, the Q ships, and received the D.S.O. for sinking the German submarine U27. Towards the end of that year he had returned to submarines to command E22; and on 25 April, 1916, a U-boat torpedoed her in the North Sea. But less than a week earlier Herbert had left to take command of another Q ship, and to get married in London.

Though he had been posted to K13 in October 1916, he had first heard about the new class eighteen months earlier. In the spring of

27

1915 he had been called to the Admiralty to receive the Sea Lords' decision on a design he had submitted for the first human torpedo. It was an idea which he had nursed since 1909. He called this device the *Devastator*. Their Lordships turned it down. After giving Herbert this dispiriting news, Commodore Hall, the new Flag Officer (Submarines), tried to hearten him with a titbit straight from the top-secret file: the Admiralty was considering a new class of submersible steam-driven destroyers. With the *Archimède* experience still fresh in his mind, Herbert was not enthusiastic. He said, 'I trust, sir, that I'll never be told to command one of them.'

But he had to admit to himself now that K13 looked impressive. She was 339 feet long and displaced on the surface 1,800 tons, figures greater than those of the latest destroyers. Her submerged displacement was 2,600 tons. Unlike most submarines, she showed a good deal of herself above her waterline. Her bows stood straight and sharp, nine feet out of the water, with a position for a 4-inch gun on the foredeck. Behind her high, streamlined conning-tower was a raised superstructure carrying a 3-inch gun and the two stubby funnels, each five feet high. Another 4-inch gun stood beyond the superstructure. In addition to her twin 30-foot periscopes, the largest yet made in Britain, she carried two tall, retractable wireless masts. With all this top-hamper and her great length, it seemed incredible to the knowledgeable Clydesiders that she could dive, and nothing short of fantastic when she surfaced again.

In all there were nine watertight doors and, apart from the torpedo tubes, twelve hatches and innumerable valves, manholes and other openings in the hull: 'too many damned holes', as more than one submariner observed. Experienced submarine captains like Herbert found that controlling a K boat bore little comparison with their previous commands. In earlier types of submarine a captain could keep watch personally on the controls and the crew. But the huge K boat had to be commanded largely by remote control: by indicators, by voice-pipes, by telephone.

The boat was divided into nine compartments: the bow torpedo-room, the officers' quarters, the control-room (which contained a wireless cabin, four feet by nine), the beam torpedo-room (from which torpedoes were fired broadside), the boiler-room, the turbine-room, the diesel engine and electric motor room, the crew space, and the steering compartment (which included further crew space). The boiler-room effectively split the submarine into two parts, linked only by the narrow boiler-room passage. There was no underwater escape apparatus.

The K was a double-hulled submarine, with a cylindrical inner or pressure hull and an outer hull of light plating. The lower half of the space between the two hulls was divided into twenty main external ballast tanks, the 'externals.' Along the bottom of the submarine, within the pressure hull, were further tanks: main ballast, A,B,C,D,Q,X,Y; auxiliary ballast, 1,2,3,4,5,6,7,8; and the fore and aft trimming tanks. The complexity of the submarine called for a high degree of crew-training.

K13 was not, of course, the first K boat to be completed, though she was the first to appear on the Clyde. K3, the keel of which King George V had laid at Vickers's yard at Barrow, had been commissioned on 4 August, 1916, only fourteen months after the signing of the contract. Of the other twelve boats which were ordered in 1915, all but one were either nearing completion or, like K13, undergoing trials. Incredibly, the Admiralty had ordered seven more between January and August of 1916: three from Vickers, two from Armstrong Whitworth and one each from the Clyde yards of Scott and Beardmore. Without tests on a prototype, the Navy was now committed to twenty-one warships of the most revolutionary design, costing more than £6,000,000. But there was nothing to worry about, the designer said: the K boat could not be faulted. From the Clyde to Plymouth, on the Tyne and in the harbours of Barrow and Portsmouth, nautical eyes boggled at the sudden appearance of the huge, twin-funnelled submarines. And in the Grand Fleet the flag officers confidently expected to be equipped with two flotillas of their new secret weapon before the spring.

What many of them did not know, and what Herbert and his crew lunching on the Gareloch certainly did not know, was that K3 was not giving the new class an auspicious start. During her surface speed trials the temperature in the boiler and turbine rooms had become unbearable even with the hatches opened wide. She took a hammering from a head sea which smashed and cracked the windows of the wheelhouse, the uppermost part of the conning-tower. To add insult to injury, a British patrol boat fired on her as she steamed off the Isle of Man. The shots happily fell short, and K3 hastily retreated, streaming black smoke.

Before K3's diving trials Commodore Hall had confided to one of his submarine captains, Lieutenant-Commander Robert Ross-Turner, 'What on earth can we do with these K boats if they won't dive?' The question never required an answer, but K3 soon showed a fickle nature under water. On one of several occasions on which parties of important people visited the submarine, the captain, Commander Edward W. Leir, had welcomed on board the future King George VI

29

accompanied by the Commander-in-Chief Portsmouth. Leir took the party for a submerged run in Stokes Bay. The Prince, then twenty-one years old, went aft on the motor control platform, escorted by Sub-Lieutenant Laurence Foley. As Leir trimmed the submarine she suddenly put her bows down at a steep angle and dived. Many men fell. Others crashed against the bulkheads. The Prince and Foley clung to handholds as K3 hit the sea-bed and burrowed her bows in the mud. With the water at this point only 150 feet deep, her stern reared above the surface, propellers spinning in the air. It took twenty minutes to free the submarine and bring her to the surface.

Later, in dry dock, her bows were inspected and the gravel dug out of her bow torpedo tubes. On her return to sea she joined the Grand Fleet at Scapa Flow. Her captain, Leir, a man with a face like Mr Punch and a matching sense of humour, dipped her funnels in salute as she passed Beatty's flagship in the harbour. The flag officers were not amused.

From Scapa she had been sent on patrols in the North Sea. On the morning of 9 January, 1917 – twenty days before K13's acceptance trials – K3 suffered another embarrassing mishap. While steaming at 10 knots with a fresh to strong breeze on her port beam, she shipped a sea down both funnels. It extinguished both boiler fires. The boat broached to, and more water cascaded down the funnels. The boiler-room became two-thirds full of water before the funnels and hatches could be closed. The auxiliary diesel engine, which Lord Fisher had visualised partly as a safety device, proved invaluable in getting the submarine safely to harbour. Commander Leir reported the accident to the commander-in-chief of the Grand Fleet and to the Admiralty, saying that he considered repetitions could be prevented 'with the experience gained'.

By this time K13 and three others of the class, K2 at Portsmouth, K4 at Barrow, and K6 at Devonport, were in the trials stage, and all excepting Herbert's boat, which had at no time to leave the relative calm of the Clyde, were experiencing difficulties similar to those which had affected K3. K13 had given no hint of serious trouble. True, the men working on her called her a holy terror, but only because she had a mischievous jinx which wrapped two ropes round her propellers and caused similar minor irritations. It was a jinx readily connected with her number, thirteen. But it had cast no doubt on her seaworthiness or performance. At her official speed trials on 18 January she had achieved 23½ knots; and the day before that she had dived and remained satisfactorily submerged in the Gareloch for an hour. By lunch on 29 January, therefore, with Herbert soon to sign the acceptance forms, the directors and works managers of the Fairfield company, who had little experience of building submarines but had completed the revolutionary K boat in fifteen months, had every reason to be pleased with themselves. Shipbuilders have a tradition of affording handsome hospitality to their guests at acceptance trials, and in spite of wartime conditions lunch in the *Comet* was no exception. The meal ended, in the pleasant aroma of cigar smoke, at 3.15 p.m.

Some minutes earlier Engineer-Lieutenant Lane, still preoccupied with the boiler-room ventilators, had asked his chief engine-room artificer to examine them again. The Chief E.R.A delegated the task to the chief stoker, who reported that the ventilators were fully open. Men at Lane's table remembered afterwards that he seemed pleased with the information.

Eighty men reboarded K13 for the final dive. Two directors of Fairfield's, Alexander Cleghorn and Macmillan, stayed in the *Comet* to go ashore at Shandon to make arrangements by telephone for dry-docking the submarine early the next morning.

Before getting under way Herbert signalled his intention to dive to another new submarine, E50, which was also undergoing acceptance trials in the loch. She came from the yard of John Brown and Company. Her captain, Lieutenant-Commander Kenneth Michell, was a close friend of Herbert. Before the war they had taken part in a remarkable surface voyage by three C-class submarines. Under escort and frequently in tow, the tiny coastal submarines had sailed 10,000 miles from Portsmouth to Hong Kong in three months. It was the sort of hazardous experience which creates strong bonds between men. Only a week or two ago Herbert had met Michell again and shown him over his new charge. With their wives, they had a wild reunion celebration in Glasgow.

When Michell received Herbert's signal he was lying about a mile away down the loch. He watched K13 parting company from the *Comet*.

Herbert headed her on the electric motors closer inshore, then turned her towards the head of the loch, and from the conning-tower passed the order 'Diving stations'. As the diving hooter blew he walked aft along the superstructure to repeat the order personally down the open engine-room hatch and to watch the funnels being lowered. Electric motors swung them on hinges into wells in the super-structure, closed by hatches which operated in unison with the funnels. The holes where the funnels passed through the pressure hull were closed by hatches worked by motors and clipped by hand from inside the submarine.

31

Herbert returned to the conning-tower. In the control-room below a red light came on, illuminating the word 'Shut'. Lieutenant Singer called out, 'Engine-room shut off.' The report was relayed up the conning-tower. Herbert ordered half speed ahead on both motors and the flooding of all but four of the main external ballast tanks. With a final glance along the upper deck, he clambered down the conning-tower, closing the hatch behind him. Stubbing out the end of his lunchtime cigar, he noticed the red light of the engine-room indicator: it was too bright and conspicuous to miss.

While the captain had been on the superstructure one of his two passengers from the sister ship K14, Lieutenant (E) Leslie Rideal, walked aft from the control-room through the passage alongside the boiler-room to watch Lane and his men at work. He went through the turbine-room and found Lane in the engine-room operating the gear which lowered the after funnel. Glancing around, Rideal noticed a light flickering in one of the electrical indicators connected to the boiler-room ventilators. The light was supposed to shine steadily when the mushroom hatches were closed. Rideal asked Lane about the flickering. Lane replied that the electrical circuit had been connected the wrong way round. Nothing more was said about it.

Lane called out, 'Close engine-room hatch.' A seaman carried out the order.

Fairfield's assistant manager on K13, a Govan man named William Struthers, poked his head through the door into the turbine-room and heard Lane saying that he did not know if the boiler-room ventilators had closed properly. Struthers promptly sought the E.R.A. responsible for the ventilators and got his assurance that he had set the control valve in the closed position.

In the control-room Herbert watched the bows of the submarine through the periscope. He flooded the remaining four external ballast tanks, and when she was trimmed down straight and steady he ordered, 'Dive 20 feet.' The hydroplanes were set to diving angles, and she slid beneath the surface. At least five minutes had passed since Herbert sent the crew to diving stations. K13 was making the third dive of her career in slow time.

In the engine-room Lieutenant Lane sent his Chief E.R.A. into the boiler-room to see whether it was leaking again. The boilers had not been worked since before lunch, and now that the room had been ventilated there would be no discomfort or danger for a man going in there. The E.R.A. closed the door behind him. Suddenly he re-appeared, calling out, 'The boiler-room is flooding freely, sir.' He slammed and clipped the watertight door.

Lieutenant Rideal saw water spouting from an exhaust-pipe leading from the boiler-room. He started forward to tell the captain what was happening. He hurried across the turbine-room, and in the passage alongside the boiler-room squeezed by Edward Hepworth, the Admiralty's boiler overseer. Hepworth had been watching the boiler-room through a bull's-eye window in the side of the passage. He was rushing aft to tell them in the engine-room that water was streaming through the fans which hung below the ventilators. But as he got there Lane was already calling out, 'Tell the captain to surface at once. The boiler-room is flooding.'

The man stationed at the voice-pipe repeated the message.

Hepworth turned back towards the control-room.

A moment or two later Struthers, the Fairfield assistant manager, followed him. In the passage he stopped to peer through the bull's-eye. To his horror he saw water surging more than half-way up the bulkheads of the boiler-room. He glanced back towards the turbine-room. Water was swirling along the passage towards his feet. He ran forward.

Only seconds after Herbert at the periscope had watched the bows go under water a seaman at the voice-pipes rapped out, 'Surface at once. The boiler-room is flooding.'

'Hard to rise!' Herbert shouted. 'Blow two and three!'

The depth gauge indicated ten feet as the operators spun the hydroplane wheels and compressed air hissed into the forward tanks. Still she went down. Fifteen feet. Twenty feet . . . The coxswain, Chief Petty Officer Oscar Moth, called out, 'She's out of control, sir.'

A blast of warm air swept from the after compartments into the control-room. The men's ears became oppressed by a sharp increase in air pressure; and now they knew the enormity of the inrush.

'Close watertight doors.'

'Drop forward keel.'

'Blow all forward tanks.'

Herbert snapped out the orders. The rating at the engine-room voice-pipe relayed them aft. In the bow half of the submarine men leaped to obey. A seaman pulled the handle releasing the forward of the two ten-ton keels, both of which could be dropped in an emergency. Other men closed the vents on the number one tanks and opened the compressed air valves. Still K13 sank. Singer flung himself at the after door in the control-room. It would not shut. Coming from aft, Rideal pushed his way through and turned to help the lieutenant. They slammed the door into position seconds before Hepworth, the boiler overseer, reached it. Cut off in the amidships torpedo-room, he rushed back to close the door into the boiler-room passage. Struthers, coming along the passage, saw the door shutting and hurled himself through the gap. A second later would have been too late.

On the surface of the loch Kenneth Michell, from the conning-tower of E50, saw nothing abnormal in the submergence of K13, except, perhaps, that she went under rather quickly. Immediately after she disappeared he and the men with him noticed two round specks on the water. From a mile away they assumed that the tips of the periscopes had momentarily broken the surface again. But on the shore in front of the Shandon Hydropathic Hotel one of the housemaids, Annie MacIntyre, having watched the submarine diving from a much closer position, saw the two objects in the water and recognised them as the heads of men who cried out, then vanished. Annie ran into the hotel and told people what she had seen, but no one believed her. For a long time, even when it was known that K13 had foundered, no one believed her.

Stern first, the submarine came gently to rest on the bottom, about 50 feet down, listing slightly to port and inclined four degrees up by the bows. The men still alive in her stared disbelievingly at one another, expecting the compressed air hissing into the tanks to send her shooting to the surface at any moment. 'Stop both motors,' Herbert commanded. As he spoke three thick spouts of water shot out of the voice-pipes from the after compartments, dowsing a number of men and spraying the port switchboard. The stop-valves to the pipes lay behind the wireless cabin, some within easy reach, others almost inaccessible. Before anyone could reach the valves, fuses at the back of the board began to blow. Electric cables crackled and smoked, then burst into flame. Some of the lighting circuits failed. Men tried to smother the fires with their bare hands, with caps, with sacks, with pieces torn from overalls. Electric shocks threw them back. Someone smashed the drawer from the chart table into sticks to poke wet sacking on to the burning switchboard. The fire was using precious oxygen, and polluting the air with dense, foul-smelling white smoke. Choking, half-blinded and painfully deafened by the high air pressure, the men fought to put it out, ignoring cuts and burns. A young man from Pembrokeshire, William Hancock, the Admiralty's electrical overseer, smashed his wrist-watch and tore his arm as he beat at the switchboard with his bare hands.

Another man was trying to plug two of the voice-pipes with his bare hands. At last someone rammed pieces of sacking into them and largely staunched the flow.

A sharp tapping noise came from the after bulkhead of the control-room. Herbert ordered that the door into the amidships torpedo-room

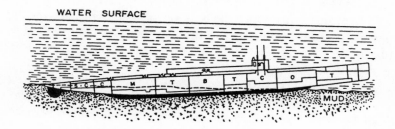

The position of K13 at the bottom of Gareloch

be opened, cautiously. Distraught and breathless, Struthers and Hepworth stepped through the doorway. 'All aft of the torpedo-room is flooded', Struthers said. Herbert tried to telephone Lane. The line was dead.

The floor of the torpedo-room itself was still largely dry, but water was spraying from a number of leaks where electric cables, telegraph and steering-rods and voice-pipes passed aft through sleeves in the bulkhead. Like the bulkheads throughout the submarine, this one separating the torpedo-room from the boiler-room was built to withstand pressures not exceeding 15 pounds to the square inch; it was now bearing, at a depth of 55 feet in the loch, nearly 25 pounds to the square inch. How long it would continue to do so Herbert did not dare to think. It was reasonable to assume that bulkheads beyond the boiler-room had already collapsed, that the compartments were flooded, and the men in them drowned. Herbert grimly ordered all the remaining intact fuses in the after circuits of the submarine to be withdrawn. The effect was to deprive the after compartments of light and power, but he was certain that by now there was no need for either. For those left alive in the forward half, the conserving of power and the prevention of further fires were of prime importance.

There was time now to take stock of the situation. The water from the voice-pipes had run away into the bilges, but the control-room and officers' quarters stank with the fumes of the burnt cables. Though some of the electric circuits had failed, there was ample power for lighting, pumping and compressing, because the batteries, which lay under the decking of the control-room and the officers' quarters, the next compartment forward, had been charged fully during the week-end. Herbert decided nevertheless to maintain the lighting at a minimum to conserve the current.

The reserves of compressed air were running low. The air was stored in four-foot-long metal cylinders called bottles. The dive that morning had taken about half the supply; and now they had used considerable quantities in trying to make the submarine rise. The after groups of bottles were unfortunately controlled by valves in the engine-room. Similarly, they could not shed the after ten-ton keel because it was controlled from the engine-room.

As a first step Herbert ordered Singer to send a distress call to E50 on the Fessenden, a crude underwater signalling device in use at that time. Meanwhile Struthers, seeing the leaking voice-pipes stuffed with sacking, told the captain that he knew the exact location of the stop-valves. Two men lifted him so that he could reach across the top of the wireless cabin and turn them off. Singer reported that the Fessenden would not work.

Herbert asked the manager of Fairfield's electrical department, Edward Skinner, and Hancock, to set about rewiring the key circuits, particularly the forward bilge pump, which was needed to keep down the water in the amidships torpedo-room. Robert Lake, the eighteen-year-old representative of Brotherhood's, the Peterborough engineering firm, got the high-pressure air compressor working, so that some of the air in the submarine could be drawn into the air bottles. Herbert's object here was twofold: to reduce the pressure which was causing several men extreme pain in their ears, and to conserve some relatively fresh air for later use. At the same time the reduction of the pressure undoubtedly had the unwelcome effect of increasing the strain on the bulkhead which was separating the trapped men from the Gareloch.

At this point a roll-call was taken.

In addition to Herbert, Singer, Rideal, Struthers, Hepworth, Lake, Skinner, and Hancock, those answering were:

Frederick W. Searle, the Admiralty ship overseer;

Frederick C. Cocks, of the Admiralty's construction department;

Donald Renfrew and Sidney Black, of Kelvin, Bottomley and Baird, the navigation equipment makers;

William Wallace, a director of Brown Brothers and Company, the Edinburgh boiler-makers;

Captain Joseph Duncan, a Clyde pilot, in his sixties and the oldest man aboard, who had taken the assignment mainly 'to have his first dive in a submarine';

William McLean, Fairfield's submarine manager;

Donald Hood, a leading hand at Fairfield's engine department;

Frank Bullen, like Struthers an assistant manager on K13 during her building;

John Green, Fairfield's head foreman mechanic;

Henry Kerr, his assistant;

Professor Percy Hillhouse, naval architect at Fairfield's;

Edward Powney, of Chadburn's, the Liverpool marine equipment firm;

Commander Francis Goodhart, captain of K14;

Chief Petty Officer Oscar Moth; and twenty-six naval ratings.

Total: forty-nine.

Those not answering the call, in addition to Lieutenant Lane, were:

Frederick Hole, assistant to Searle, the overseer;

John Steel and William Smith, foremen in the Fairfield engine department;

Frank Neate, assistant to Skinner; William Lewis, William Strachan and William Kirk, all leading hands in the Fairfield engine department; and twenty-three naval ratings.

Total: thirty-one.

During the first hour of the accident Herbert repeatedly called the engine-room on the telephone: it was a gesture made more out of an unwillingness to accept that the men aft were dead than out of hope that anyone would answer.

The trapped men began to discuss their chances of survival. They searched first for factors in their favour. The captain had dived the submarine in shallow water soon after high tide: at low water they would be only 43 feet from the surface. Captain Duncan, the pilot, assured everyone that the submarine was lying on clean, hard gravel, which would make the divers' task easier. And, of course, the resources of the greatest shipbuilding and engineering centre in the world lay only a few miles away.

But the items standing against their chances of survival looked the more conclusive. They had submerged at 3 p.m., and unless the *Comet* or E50 had noticed anything exceptional about the dive, no one on the surface would become seriously alarmed until about 3.30. Dusk would set in rapidly at four, so they could not reasonably expect any contact with would-be rescuers until daybreak tomorrow at seven. This would mean waiting for at least sixteen hours, always provided that the air-supply held out, that the bulkheads stood firm and that the pump continued to work.

Hillhouse, the naval architect, a characteristically imperturbable scientist complete with his slide rule, calculated the quantity of air available to them. They were trapped in an area 124 feet long, generally 8 feet high and tapering in width from 20 feet to 6 feet. There was, he estimated, approximately 12,000 cubic feet of air space. This gave each of the 48 men an average of about 250 cubic feet of air. Now, about 20 per cent of air is oxygen, but a man cannot survive if the proportion falls below 16 per cent. In other words, if he has only a fixed quantity of air he will start to suffocate as soon as he reduces the oxygen content by 4 per cent. In K13, therefore, each man could reckon that 4 per cent of his 250 cubic-foot ration of air separated him from death. Ten cubic feet of oxygen between him and his coffin. Ten cubic feet would just about fill a coffin.

Hillhouse diligently continued his calculations. A man resting breathes about two-thirds of a cubic foot of oxygen in an hour. If all the men in the submarine could lie still they could expect to live for fifteen hours. If they had to work the consumption of oxygen would rise steeply. Hard work multiplies the oxygen intake nine times. As most of the men had nothing to do, Hillhouse reckoned that each would use oxygen at an average rate of 1¼ cubic feet an hour. Explaining his arithmetic and his assumptions to Herbert, he said that they could expect the air to support life for eight hours, or half-way through the night.

At the captain's request and making further use of his slide rule, Hillhouse examined the chances of surfacing the submarine. It did not take him long to report that even if Herbert could blow every drop of water out of the forward ballast tanks the bows would not rise. Herbert and his fellow-captain, Goodhart, concluded that, even in the unlikely event of their surviving till divers found the submarine, 'nothing short of blowing off the after part will bring us to the surface'.

The information from Hillhouse's calculations passed from man to man.

Hepworth walked over to the professor and said quietly, expressing the thoughts of them all, 'This looks like the end'.

'I'm afraid it is', Hillhouse said.

Petty Officer Moth, who had run the gauntlet of the Dardanelles in the E-class submarine not many months before, said aloud, to no one in particular but with vehement disgust, 'What a bloody rotten way to die'.

CHAPTER THREE

AN EXAMPLE OF 'BAD SALVAGE'

His Majesty the King heartily congratulates survivors of K13 on their marvellous escape . . . – Admiralty signal, 31 January, 1917.

T he men on the conning-tower of E50, watching the submergence of K13, had their attention caught first by the two round objects in the water and then, seconds later, by a disturbance on the surface. It looked from a distances like a large escape of air. Lieutenant-Commander Michell had planned to dive his submarine once more before returning to John Brown's yard, but now the behaviour of Herbert's boat intrigued him, and after a while he ordered slow ahead and moved with caution near to the spot where K13 had dived. He expected her to break the surface at any moment.

The light was fading quickly. It was strange, Michell felt, that Herbert, practically a bridegroom, was not already making tracks for home. He put out E50's collapsible skiff and, with two ratings, rowed over the area where the disturbance occurred. Streams of bubbles broke the surface all around. There were small streaks of oil. K13 was obviously below, in trouble. Michell took a sample of the water, wondering if the conning-tower hatch had not closed properly and water had flooded the batteries. But back on E50 he could not detect acid in the water. He felt reassured. A new submarine could easily overtrim and sink to the bottom. In the comparatively shallow water K13 would have come to no harm. As soon as Herbert blew the excess water from the tanks, Michell told himself, he would have her under control again.

The *Comet* returned from Shandon pier, bearing the two Fairfield directors, Cleghorn and Macmillan, both of whom had seen the eruption on the surface after K13 had gone under. Michell reassured them on the basis of his inspection and from his knowledge of Herbert. 'He's fond of doing the unexpected', he told them. Michell remembered vividly the stunts Herbert had performed with one of the C boats after

39

their historic voyage to Hong Kong before the war. He had stood on the conning-tower hatch of C36, clinging to the periscope and venti-lator tube, while the crew submerged her to the point where the water lapped at his feet and he appeared to be sliding across the sea. Herbert had repeated the manoeuvre more recently on wartime patrols in the Channel with D5. He claimed that on moonlit summer nights it made the submarine virtually invisible and allowed him to aim and fire torpedoes at enemy vessels without wasting precious seconds in diving. It was an experiment which Herbert was never able to put to the test; it was also a feat of submarine skill and crew training which prompted Michell to tell the Fairfield directors that the captain of K13 was one of the most capable submarine officers he knew.

The minutes moved by, and only the streams of bubbles broke the darkening water. By four o'clock the dusk blackened into night, and Michell, now alarmed, decided to anchor. He sent his first lieutenant ashore to telephone the senior naval officer of the Clyde, asking for salvage plant of all available types to be sent as fast as possible. Cleghorn simultaneously called the Fairfield yard to report what had happened and to ask for help.

Over the Gareloch the air turned icy. Michell sent a party in E50's skiff to patrol above K13's position lest anything or anyone came to the surface. He was puzzled: why had his hydrophones received no signals from the other submarine's Fessenden device? Michell cursed the Admiralty department which earlier in the war had turned down as dangerous his suggestion that submarines should carry telephone buoys. In such an emergency as this the men in the submarine could have released the buoy and spoken to him. But the Admiralty feared that a buoy might have been released accidentally, revealing a sub-marine's presence to the enemy. Michell had maintained unsuccessfully that the buoys should at least be fitted during trials: but the idea was not adopted until the 1930s, many submarine disasters later.

Down in K13, the men discovered that they could not open the watertight door between the two most forward compartments, the officers' quarters and the bow torpedo-room. A clip on the forward side of the door had dropped accidentally into place when the door had been shut in response to Herbert's order. No one had stayed in the torpedo-room, so no one could lift the clip. Yet access to the room might prove vital, both for the air it contained and as a possible escape route. Four of the civilians, McLean, Struthers, Green and Bullen, set to work to force the door. They stripped away the watertight rubber packing, and after more than two hours, with sweat glistening on their faces, they created enough play in the door to raise the clip with a piece of bent wire. The door swung open to a loud cheer from the rest of the men.

In the amidships torpedo-room water pouring through the glands in the bulkhead, rose at the rate of two feet an hour. The electric bilge pump kept the level down.

Occasionally lights fused as water crept into the circuits. Skinner and Hancock were kept busy rewiring. At the time of the sinking the hydraulic system, which raised the periscopes and wireless masts, was operating on the after pump in the engine-room. One of the contractors' representatives, William Wallace, a young director of a boiler-making firm in Edinburgh, set about reconnecting it to the forward pump. A newly married man, Wallace was lucky to be alive. All morning since the steering mishap in the Clyde he had stayed aft to ensure that no one switched off the gear again accidentally. Only since lunch had he stopped in the control-room to watch the diving procedure. To blank off the hydraulic system in the stern half of the boat he broke the pipe leading aft and jammed into it a two-shilling piece. Herbert then ordered that the forward wireless mast be raised in the hope that it would break the surface of the loch and reveal the submarine's precise position.

By eight o'clock most of the men resigned themselves to a night of waiting and perhaps of dying. The realists occupied themselves by writing farewell notes. The young Welshman, Hancock, wrote a note to his parents and stuffed it in a bottle which he corked and put in his pocket.

There were sufficient sandwiches on board to allow a ration of one and a half rounds to each man; but no one felt hungry. The shortage of air and its foulness from the smoke made everyone thirsty; but the sea had polluted the fresh-water tank. The icy water of the Gareloch drew the heat out of the submarine, and the men shivered and some huddled together for warmth. The electric power was too precious to waste on the radiators. Duncan, the pilot, kept warm and occupied himself by striding up and down the control-room floor, as if he were still in command on the bridge of a surface ship. Someone had pointed out to him that this activity wasted oxygen, but he was a law unto himself.

Meanwhile, in Glasgow, Mrs Herbert telephoned the Fairfield Shipbuilding Company to find out why her husband was late for dinner. Someone tactfully told her that the minor collision in the Clyde in the morning had delayed the submarine's trials. An hour or so later, when two naval officers called at the Herberts' lodgings to tell Mrs

Herbert of the accident, she cut them short, saying it was good of them to call but she had already heard about the trouble. The two men left amazed at the aplomb of the captain's wife, without telling her that K13 was on the bottom of the Gareloch.

Much confusion at first slowed the arrangements for rescuing the men in K13. At the Navy's Clyde headquarters and at the Fairfield works, the senior men had gone home when the first emergency telephone calls came from the Shandon hotel. Not until well after ten o'clock did the first rescue vessel, an old gunboat named *Gossamer*, leave her berth at Greenock for the Gareloch. At eleven o'clock Alexander Gracie, the chairman of the Fairfield company, and Acting Captain Godfrey Corbett, assistant to the senior naval officer on the Clyde, left by car for Shandon, twenty-seven miles from Glasgow. At 10.56 p.m., seven hours after the accident, the Admiralty in London first heard about it in a coded signal:

> Submarine K13 on bottom off Shandon in Gareloch details not yet known am sending salvage vessels Tay and Thrush and two large hoppers with wires etc. Depth of water (?) 12 fathoms Captain Corbett is at Shandon in charge of operations will report in the morning.

Corbett and Gracie in fact arrived at Shandon at midnight to find *Gossamer* and E50 standing by the suspected scene of the accident. The gunboat had two boats out with a sweep wire, grappling somewhat uselessly for K13. They made contact with what was obviously the submarine at about 2 a.m. The exercise merely helped to prove what Michell already knew: that K13 was below the spot where the bubbles still rose.

Gossamer carried a diving-suit, but no diver. Gracie sent his chauffeur back to Glasgow to fetch Fairfield's own diver. He was not at home. At four in the morning the car returned to Shandon with the diver's young assistant. On *Gossamer* he donned the diving-suit and stepped into the water. No sooner had he submerged than the suit, which had not been used for years, burst. He was pulled half-drowned out of the water. Once more the Fairfield car raced back to Glasgow, to collect another suit.

Two more rescue ships arrived: a trawler and an old sloop named *Thrush*, commanded by Lieutenant Ivor Kay, came straight from towing a mined steamer into harbour, and as a result was short of gear. She had neither a diver nor a diving-suit on board.

In Glasgow Elizabeth Herbert waited until well past twelve o'clock for her husband, then went to bed convinced that the submarine had anchored for the night somewhere in the Clyde estuary. She was

42

roused shortly before seven o'clock by her landlady knocking at the door. Several wives of the crew of K13 had called at the house, inquiring about their menfolk. Mrs Herbert telephoned the Fairfield yard and learned that there had been 'a wee accident on the Gareloch'. Her informant would say no more. She comforted the women as best she could, then hurried to the Central Hotel where Mrs Goodhart was living. The two women repeatedly telephoned the shipyard, but no one would give them details of the accident. The office of the senior naval officer on the Clyde had ordered the strictest secrecy.

On the road running alongside the Gareloch the car was returning to Shandon with another diving-suit. Soon after daybreak the young Fairfield diver, none the worse for his earlier experience, made a second descent. Michell told him to walk along the hull of the submarine, tapping as he went to discover whether anyone was alive. As soon as he landed on the deck of K13 the men on the surface heard the tapped responses from the entombed men as clearly as if the submarine had been a few feet away instead of seven fathoms under water. Michell passed down a lead line, and while the diver guided it on to the hull of the submarine a signaller in the skiff with Michell tapped out a question in Morse code. The men in K13 immediately replied: ALL WELL BEFORE ENGINE-ROOM BULKHEAD. Inexplicably, that was the only successful exchange of messages tapped in Morse. The men on the surface could not read the replies to their subsequent questions.

Nor in K13 could the trapped men always read the questions tapped from the surface. The concentration of carbonic acid in the air had begun slowly to drug them. One per cent of carbon dioxide in the air causes breathlessness; at 3 per cent, the breathlessness becomes painful; at 5 per cent all exertion becomes impossible. Already some of the men were breathing rapidly. During the night they had greeted the sound of the sweep wire scraping over the hull with a wild, expectant cheer. But now many of them were indifferent to the stomping of the diver's heavy boots and the tapping of the lead line. They lay inert on the deck. For warmth two, sometimes three, men crammed into each of the berths in the officers' quarters. Others shared the comfort of the one armchair. A number of men found standing more comfortable. The indomitable river pilot still paced up and down.

At intervals Skinner nursed the bilge pump into action to clear the amidships torpedo-room, and McLean forced some of the vitiated air into the air bottles while releasing fresher air from other bottles. Young Lake and Bullen tended the high-pressure compressors, and Hancock patched the lighting circuits.

43

At daybreak Herbert raised the periscope and at first thought it had cleared the surface of the Gareloch. He saw a picture of a light green sunlit sea with a man rowing in a small boat. But the men and the boat did not move. The head of the periscope was under water, and specks on the prisms created the illusion. It was obvious that the sun was shining brightly, for even 40 feet below the surface Herbert could see through the bull's-eye windows in the sides of the conning-tower the wire guard-rail around the main deck of K13.

During much of the early morning Herbert and Goodhart had talked privately in the captain's cabin about ways of escape. They feared that their rescuers would concentrate too much on raising K13, and not enough on keeping its occupants alive. Somehow they had to be told that it was more important at this stage to fix air and food supply lines to valves in the hull. Herbert, bound as captain to be the last to leave his vessel, asking Goodhart to try to reach the surface. It was possible, though highly dangerous, to leave the submarine through the conning-tower. Goodhart agreed to do it.

The conning-tower proper, a brass casting, was a small compartment within the bridge structure of the submarine. It was reached from the control-room through a watertight hatch which opened upwards. In horizontal section the tower was oval-shaped, 5 ft 6 in. long and 3 ft 6 in. at its widest point. The after portion of the tower was 4 ft 6 in. high, and contained a hatch opening upwards into the chart-room. The forward portion was 3 ft. 6 in. higher, and formed a dome, in which were an electric light and the submarine's projector compass. Here, in this non-magnetic compartment, the compass was beyond the influence of the steelwork of the main hull.

Herbert and Goodhart planned to enter the conning-tower together, and, after the men below had clipped the lower hatch, to unfasten the upper hatch and open a sea valve. As the water rose in the tower it would squeeze the air upwards until its pressure became equal to that of the sea-water outside. Standing with their hands in the dome, from which the air could escape, Herbert and Goodhart would then open the upper hatch. When water occupied all the space below the dome Herbert would turn on a high-pressure air valve, Goodhart would duck through the upper hatch, and, helped by the high-pressure air, try to find his way through the flooded chart-room to the surface. Herbert would then shut off the air, close and clip the upper hatch and knock loudly on the floor of the conning-tower with an iron rod. At this signal the men in the control-room would open a valve to drain the water from the tower. Herbert would simultaneously let in a small amount of compressed air to replace the water. With the tower empty again, the men below would unfasten the hatch and Herbert would rejoin them.

The two men timed the attempt for midday, at low tide. They worked through the morning removing the projector compass and most of its tube to give themselves room in the conning-tower. Where the tube passed down into the control-room the Fairfield men fixed a flexible hose which they led into the amidships torpedo-room. After Goodhart had left they would drain the conning-tower through this hose. To give Herbert a high-pressure air supply, they used a voice-pipe. They fitted a lead from the air system to the end of the pipe in the control-room, then broke the pipe at a joint in the conning-tower. Below the break they fitted a valve. Finally, they made a seacock out of the fuel vent pipe. The pipe led from below, through a valve, then out through the side of the conning-tower. The Fairfield men cut away part of the pipe below the valve so that, when the valve was opened, the sea would pour in.

Herbert tested the tower for leaks by charging it with high-pressure air. The lower hatch was tight, but air hissed from some of the glands through which electric cables passed. It took an hour to seal them off.

With everything ready, Herbert wrote a brief description of what had happened, of the conditions in the boat and of what he felt the would-be rescuers ought to do. Lieutenant Singer compiled a list of men alive in the boat. These notes, with several farewell messages, were pushed into a 10-inch tin cylinder in which Professor Hillhouse had carried his hydrometer. Goodhart was to release the cylinder, decked in red bunting as soon as he got clear of the wheelhouse. 'Well, if I don't get up', he said, picking up the cylinder and putting it under his belt, 'this will.' If he did reach the surface he was to arrange for divers to tap a signal on the hull of the submarine.

Both men wore a shirt, trousers and socks. Herbert put on his sea-boots to weight himself down. Both men handed their jackets to seamen suffering from the cold. Herbert gave his wrist-watch to the second coxswain. 'I might ask you for that later on', he said, grinning.

At about midday the two men climbed into the conning-tower, going, so it seemed to the others, to certain and immediate death. They closed the lower hatch and the man below clipped it. Goodhart opened the sea valve. The icy water rose quickly over their feet and up their legs. Herbert noticed a prawn lodged against one of the bull's-eye windows, its black eyes pressed against the glass, staring at the light. The air compressed, and both men became painfully breathless. Their ears were drumming and deafened, and a thick fog rose and blotted out the electric light. The water reached their waists, and Herbert turned on the high-pressure air. Goodhart knocked off the clips on the upper hatch. The pressure inside and out equalised, and as air bubbled out through the hatch, water streamed in. The level rapidly rose to the bottom of the dome. Goodhart reached under and pushed the hatch wide open. He said, 'Well, I'm off', and took a deep breath. 'Good luck', Herbert shouted. Goodhart ducked under the water and shot through the hatch.

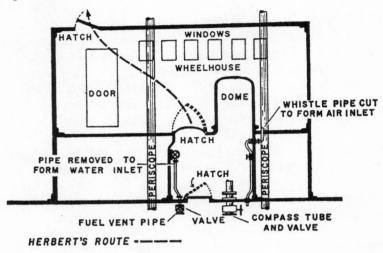

The conning-tower of K13

Almost immediately Herbert bent down and felt for the hatch to close it. The force of the expanding high pressure air took him by surprise and swept him off his feet. Next moment he found himself blown through the hatchway into the chart-room. He struck his head on the roof, but the air-stream carried him miraculously through a square flap hatch and clear of K13. Instinctively he held his hands in front of his face and breathed hard, kicking with his feet. The high-pressure air bore him upwards surrounded by bubbles.

All morning on the surface much discussion and argument had gone on about the method of rescuing the trapped men. After receiving the signal 'All well before engine-room bulkhead', Michell took E50 alongside *Gossamer* and boarded her to meet Captain Brian Bartelott, the senior naval officer of the Clyde, and a number of top executives from the Fairfield company. He sought permission to try to lift the bows of K13 clear of the water with a 6½-inch wire slung between

Thrush and the trawler, but the Fairfield men, still technically the owners of the submarine, objected strongly, saying she would break in two. They wanted to build a steel rescue tube 27 inches wide and 60 feet long, which could be lowered on to the midships torpedo hatch and caulked watertight. They said that such a tube could be pumped dry so that the hatch could be opened and the men hauled to safety.

Michell argued that it would take too long to make the tube, that its effect would be uncertain, and that they did not know if the trapped men could open the midships torpedo hatch. He urged them again to allow him to try to raise the bows with the object of rescuing the men through the four bow torpedo tubes. At this point Bartelott, assuming total responsibility for the operation, ordered Michell to carry on as he thought best. Under the direction of Lieutenant Kay, *Thrush* and the trawler immediately began a sweep with the wire and at the first attempt passed it under the bows of K13.

At about midday *Thrush* took the strain on the wire, and as the capstan turned the trawler heeled over slightly. Suddenly a tremendous surge of air turned the water between the two lifting vessels into a cauldron. For one shattering moment Michell thought K13 had broken in two. Then he saw a man coming to the surface in a huge bubble. He leaned over the side of the trawler and tried to catch the man by the seat of his trousers, but the foaming water whirled him towards the diver's boat. The diver, standing on the ladder but with his helmet off, grabbed the man and helped him aboard.

It was Herbert.

'Where's Goodhart?' he gasped.

No one knew what he was talking about.

'Where's Goodhart?' he repeated.

Someone said, 'We thought he was in K13 with you, sir.'

'I've just blown him out of the conning-tower. Haven't you seen him?'

There was an uneasy silence. Men scoured the surrounding water, and a call went across to the other boats to watch for Goodhart. They ushered the dazed and shivering Herbert on board *Thrush* and into the warmth of Lieutenant Kay's cabin. They stripped him and rubbed him down and dosed him with brandy.

Outside there was no sign of Goodhart.

Michell went abroad *Thrush*, and Herbert told him that K13 had to have compressed air as fast as possible so that the men in her could blow the forward tanks to assist the lifting operation.

'The engine-room bulkhead is leaking badly', he said, 'and the bilge pump is running on makeshift leads which might break down for good at any moment.'

47

Two more divers arrived from Greenock, and Michell brought E50 alongside the trawler so that they could begin at once to act on Herbert's advice and connect his boat's high-pressure system to an external connection on K13. Michell's coxswain, a provident man, had equipped E50 with four spare lengths of 5-inch high-pressure air hose, just sufficient to reach the sunken submarine. But unhappily the divers could not find the external connection.

The afternoon dragged by and darkness set in. Just after four o'clock Alexander Gracie, the Fairfield chairman, telephoned the Central Hotel in Glasgow to speak to Mrs Herbert. He told her that her husband was safe, but that Goodhart was missing. The two women decided to go to Shandon.

Soon after five the Naval Salvage Adviser, Captain Frederick Young, arrived at the scene of the accident from Liverpool. He approved of the steps Michell had taken; and he approved, too, of the idea of building an escape tube. Instructions for building the tube were at once telephoned to the Fairfield yard. The majority of the men had left for home, but special messengers recalled them.

In spite of the secrecy, news of the accident spread quickly round Clydeside. Crowds gathered on the shore of the Gareloch to watch the salvage ships. A tugboat arrived from Scott's shipyard at Greenock, where K15 was being built, bringing two K boat experts with plans, tools, hoses and other gear.

The air in K13 had kept the men alive now for more than twenty-four hours, some three times longer than Hillhouse had estimated. So little oxygen remained that a match when struck would not light but gave off only a puff of smoke. The men had given up hope since Herbert had failed to return from the conning-tower. They had heard the tower being flooded and the gurgling of the high-pressure air; and they had waited in vain for the thumping signal from Herbert, or for the signal from the divers that Goodhart had reached the surface. Reluctantly they closed the air valve, and assumed that both commanders had drowned.

William Wallace, the young company director from Edinburgh, proposed that he should try to reach the surface through one of the beam torpedo tubes. He reckoned that with a bottle of compressed air he could raise the pressure in the tube to that of the sea outside, then remove the outer cover and shoot himself out. But the idea was too hazardous to consider. 'It would be a waste of good air', McLean said.

By five on the Tuesday afternoon it seemed that some men would not live much longer. A number of the crew and the older civilians appeared virtually moribund as they sprawled on the deck. Lieutenant

Singer, on whom command had fallen after the disappearance of Herbert, had spent most of the time on his bunk, calling spasmodically for a cup of tea. Of course, none was available. After a while Fred Searle, the Admiralty overseer, had got the lieutenant's permission to take charge. With McLean and Bullen, Searle was so far the least affected by the conditions. Singer's state of collapse had steadily worsened. Now he was breathing rapidly, apparently in severe pain and delirium. Some thought he was dying. Young Lake was obviously serious ill, too; but he insisted on standing by the high-pressure compressor and operating it when McLean wanted to circulate the air through the air bottles. The effort of turning a valve five or six times was enough to exhaust him completely for half an hour. At intervals a fuse flashed and spat and jumped out of the switchboard; and one or more of the lights would fail. Between rewiring the fuses, Hancock amused himself by checking his rate of breathing: it had reached 170 to 180 breaths a minute. Periodically the boat's leading signalman, Arthur Riley, found the energy to hammer in Morse code on the hull: GIVE US AIR GIVE US AIR.

At one point Searle thought that William Wallace had become slightly deranged. Wallace had spent most of his idle time so far worrying about his new bridge and about the jobs he had left undone at home, but suddenly he burst into laughter at the thought of the agitation his disappearance might cause in the offices of a certain insurance company in Edinburgh. His firm always insured members of its staff for £10,000 when they went on assignments of this kind. It tickled Wallace as he imagined his office receiving repeated telephone calls from his insurers, anxious to discover whether or not they had to fork out £10,000 or not. This explanation did not, however, amuse Fred Searle. He was convinced that Wallace was a little unhinged.

Men sprawled everywhere. Their mouths and throats were parched and their tongues discoloured from thirst. The cold no longer affected them. The poisoned air effectively dulled the senses of most of them, though a few had earlier shown slight signs of panic: one in particular, the biggest man aboard, had to be felled with a spanner when he tried to open a hatch.

Not until six in the evening did the divers join the air line to the elusive connections on K13. In the meantime one of them had strapped a lamp to the submarine's forward periscope, through which he now flashed a signal to the men inside to open the appropriate valve. Bullen and McLean partly opened one of the joints in the air system below the valve, then cautiously turned the valve itself. Seawater mixed with a few bubbles streamed through the joint. Dispirited beyond words, they closed the valve, and Riley tried to tap a message on the hull to explain what was happening.

Forty-odd feet above, the apparent delay in opening the valve baffled the rescue party. E50's compressors were being driven up to 2,500 pounds a square inch, but none of the air was finding its way into K13. As the night dragged on the divers, working in bitterly cold water, placed a hydrophone on the deck of the submarine. Through it Michell and his colleagues could hear almost every movement of the trapped men. With heart-rending regularity, they picked up the signal; GIVE US AIR GIVE US AIR. But all other signals were incomprehensible. Believing that the men below had failed to open the valve, Michell had a message in Morse code blown through a Klaxon horn in an airtight drum laid on the deck of K13. But still no air passed through the hose.

By now it was one o'clock in the morning. On shore Mrs Herbert and Mrs Goodhart arrived by taxi at the Shandon Hydropathic Hotel. Herbert was in bed. He had insisted on helping the rescue party until in the end his fellow-officers had virtually to order him to the hotel to rest. His wife did not disturb him. Captain Bartelott took her on one side and asked her to break the news to Mrs Goodhart that her husband was dead.

Back on the salvage vessels, Michell decided that the only thing left to do was to make certain that the high-pressure pipe itself was not faulty. The divers, at exhaustion point after working without a break all day, went below once more and brought the lower end of the pipe to the surface. It was blocked by several inches of ice. Michell cursed and berated himself for not making a check earlier. *Seven hours wasted.*

In K13 the men still clung to life. Periodically a handful of them staggered to attend the bilge pump and the compressor. A signal through the periscope brought Bullen and McLean to their feet, once more cautiously to open the inboard air valve. Michell had cleared the pipe, and the divers had reconnected it. And this time the hissing of compressed air filled the submarine. The effect of this sound on the trapped men was immediate and remarkable. Some who had appeared semi-conscious sat up, wide-eyed. Several struggled to their feet and gathered round the air pipe. They even raised a cheer. It was thirty-five hours since K13 had gone down.

With the pressure inside the hull already high, Searle allowed only a small quantity of air to escape before he told Bullen and McLean to close the joint in the pipe and to concentrate on recharging the empty air bottles. They filled several groups of bottles to the full pressure of 2,500 pounds, then at once proceeded to blow all the ballast tanks under their control: in other words, those forward of the engine-room

50

bulkhead. In the control-room several men anxiously watched the bubbles in the fore and aft spirit-levels for some sign that the bows were lifting; but though tank after tank was emptied the bubbles remained motionless at four degrees up by the bow, as they had since K13 settled on the bottom. All but two of the tanks had been blown and the men were giving up hope when suddenly there was movement. They gave a shout of delight as the forward bubble indicated five degrees, then six . . . seven . . . eight . . . nine . . . ten . . . They could feel the submarine inclining under their feet.

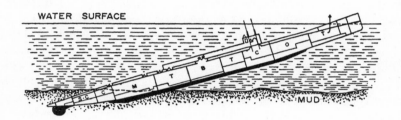

Final position of K13 with bow raised

The surface of the Gareloch became like a rough sea as the compressed air ejected the water from K13's tanks. On E50 most of the crew had turned in. Michell, an optimist, had visions of the sunken submarine coming to the surface with no one to receive her, and he ordered the men back to their posts.

As the bows of K13 rose *Thrush* and the trawler hove in on the 6½-inch wire. At 3 a.m. the forward wireless mast, bent by the keel of one of the rescue ships, and the forward periscope of the submarine broke the surface of the loch. The trawler was heeling badly under the tremendous strain on the wire, and Michell decided for the time being not to risk raising K13 any further. Her bows were now about eight feet under water. It took fifteen minutes of patient signalling on the lamp attached to the periscope to persuade the trapped men to stop blowing the air into the forward tanks. In the turbulent aerated water it was impossible for the divers to work. And Michell had a new job for them to do.

The plan was to fit on to K13 another pipeline through which the rescue party could pass food, fresh air and spoken messages. Soon after Herbert had escaped he had told one of the divers to unscrew and bring to the surface a brass plate covering a ventilator and ammunition hand-up over the officers' quarters. This ventilator and hand-up was seven inches wide and, of course, passed through both outer and inner hulls. The cover on the inner hull hinged downward. When the diver returned with the brass plate Herbert gave it to the chief engineer of the salvage ship *Thrush* and asked him to cut a hole in it and to braze over the hole one end of a long, flexible, armoured hosepipe, four inches in diameter. By coincidence a draughtsman from Fairfield's, John Lipton, had earlier had much the same idea, but he had returned to the shipyard to take the identical plate from K14, the sister ship. The engine department at the yard fitted a hose to the plate, but by the time Lipton returned with it to the Gareloch the divers were already screwing back into place the one taken from K13.

The trapped men could hear the activity on the deck above the officers' quarters, but they could not understand what was being done. They had refreshed the air a little by circulating it through the replenished air bottles, but many of them were still seriously ill and all were dazed. When Michell signalled to them to unfasten the inside hatch on the ventilator and ammunition hand-up no one understood the message. The second tube was now securely fastened to the submarine, and as soon as the men inside her opened the hatch in the wardroom they would have unlimited fresh air and food. But they could not be persuaded to open the hatch.

Perhaps those men still capable of helping themselves were preoccupied fighting the water leaking through the engine-room bulkhead. The raising of the bows had taken the bilge pump, which was in the officers' quarters, so high above the torpedo-room that it would no longer force out the water. More than anything the men feared the possibility of the salt water reaching the batteries and producing chlorine gas. They formed a line from the torpedo-room to one of the bilges which was on a level with the pump, and passed the water forward in two buckets, one of which leaked. Each man had to use one hand to hold himself in position on the sloping, greasy deck. It was a slow, fatiguing process.

After an hour McLean and Bullen hit upon a better method. Waist-deep in icy water, three members of the crew unscrewed a manhole cover on the floor of the torpedo-room. It took them two hours; it would have taken three fit men five minutes. The cover opened into an empty fuel tank, into which the water immediately drained. The men screwed the cover down again, and McLean opened the valve at the bottom of the tank and blew the water into the Gareloch with compressed air. With the tank empty and the valve closed, they again unfastened the cover; and the procedure was repeated. With unlimited compressed air, they were assured now of keeping the water from the batteries as long as they had strength to remove and replace the manhole cover.

On the surface of the loch Michell had sat for two hours in a bosun's chair slung under the bows of the trawler, signalling to the men in K13 to persuade them to open the inner cover on the ammunition hand-up. He had to work in this cold, uncomfortable position because the second pipeline reached only a few feet out of the water. He was tapping on the hull of the submarine with a lead weight on a line hanging down the pipe. At times, in desperation, he even bellowed down the pipe, 'Open-the-hatch.' But it stayed closed.

At daybreak Herbert came down from the Shandon hotel and relieved the frozen Michell. No sooner had Michell gone down into E50 for some cocoa than the men in K13 at last realised what was required of them and opened the hatch. Some water fell into the ward-room, but a good deal erupted upwards through the pipe as the compressed foul air escaped. The sudden drop in pressure made the men cry out as it tore at their eardrums. A jet of foul black vapour blew into Herbert's face and formed a small cloud over the water. The men on the salvage ships marvelled that anyone could have lived in it.

Herbert waited for the worst of the bad air to clear, then yelled down the pipe, 'Can you hear me down there?'

They could.

McLean called, 'Yes, we can hear you loud and clear.'

'How is everyone?'

'We're all holding out, but we need air badly. And water. Have you seen Commander Herbert?'

'This is Commander Herbert speaking.'

He heard them cheer at the news. He called a few words of encouragement, then passed a diver's air line down the pipe. The trapped men gathered round it and wafted the air over their faces, taking great gulps into their lungs. They had not breathed fresh air for more than forty-two hours. They tasted it and savoured it and consciously felt themselves coming back to life. They took the air line into the corners of the control-room and the officers' quarters and scavenged out the bad air. The pain in their ears left them, and they felt more comfortable; and for the first time they allowed themselves hope.

Herbert lowered a bottle of brandy down the pipe. Searle served it sparingly in a brass cover taken from an electric switch. One man in the crew said he had never drunk alcohol before: the occasion, everyone agreed, justified the lapse. Milk, coffee, chocolate and Bovril followed the brandy. The men wanted only to drink, not to eat: most of the original supply of sandwiches remained untouched.

Petty Officer Moth shouted into the pipeline, 'What about the men aft, Captain?'

Herbert said, 'The diver has had no reply to his knocking.'

'Is Commander Goodhart safe, sir?'

'No, I'm afraid not. We've seen nothing of him.' Herbert paused. 'Tell the lads to keep their spirits up. We mean to get you out.'

The conversation reminded him that the tin Goodhart carried had not been found, and he asked Moth to compile a new list of the survivors.

As the men revived, their hopes rose; and their sense of fear grew in direct proportion to their awareness and their hopes. A man keeping watch in the midships torpedo-room reported that the water was flowing much faster through the leaks in the boiler-room bulkhead. Hitherto the high air pressure had helped to stem the water and bolster the bulkhead. Now, with the drop in pressure putting an extra load on the bulkhead, as few men as possible remained in the control-room. Those who had to drain the torpedo-room opened the watertight door with caution and got the job over inside with haste.

Some time earlier, Skinner, Hancock and others had made arrangements for a retreat into the officers' quarters in case the bulkhead gave way. They had altered the wiring so that they could be independent of the main switchboard.

About eleven o'clock on the Wednesday morning a bottle of soda-water wedged itself in the food and air pipe. All efforts to free it with the pipe in position failed. The men in K13 had to close the inner hatch while the divers unscrewed the cover plate and took the entire pipe to the surface.

In the meantime Michell, the salvage officers and Fairfield executives discussed their next move. Some, including Herbert himself at this point, favoured lowering the submarine to the bottom of the loch again and awaiting the arrival of the rescue tube from Glasgow. They argued that time was on their side because they could pass unlimited air and food into K13: at least, they could as soon as the pipe was cleared. If, on the other hand, they tried to raise the bows higher she might slip backward into deeper water and out of their grasp. They had to remember that her stern was twelve feet deep in greasy mud.

Michell, terrier-like, insisted that the trapped men would not be able to fight the water much longer. 'That bulkhead may break down at any time', he said. 'And the air coming up the pipe is still foul. I can't stand over the pipe without my eyes streaming. We've only to lift her a few feet and the bow torpedo tubes will be clear of the water, and then we can bring the men out.'

He won his point. At midday *Thrush* and the trawler again hove in on the 6½-inch wire. The loch was calm and grey-green under the cold, clear sky. Those men not at the capstans peered into the water. Suddenly they saw her. The bows slowly broke the surface and like a sleepy monster reared ten feet clear of the water. Then Michell called a temporary halt. Two mud barges had recently arrived from the Clyde, and he wanted to use them to take some of the strain off the 6½-inch wire.

By this time the blocked pipe had been cleared and re-connected to K13. Michell called to the men that within an hour he hoped to bring them out through the upper bow torpedo tubes, which were now just below the surface. The barges were positioned one on each side of the submarine with two 4½-inch wires slung under her bows. Their sterns were trimmed down with sea-water ballast, and the wires were drawn taut.

Michell bellowed down the pipe, 'We're about to start lifting. Stand by to crawl out of the torpedo tubes. We'll hammer on the hull when they're clear of the water.'

There was a cheer from below. The men crowded into the two forward compartments.

At a signal from Michell the capstan on *Thrush* was put into gear and the barges began to pump out their flooded stern compartments. With one of his crew, Michell rowed the skiff to meet the first men out of the torpedo tubes. But as they passed under the bows a frenzied shout came from one of the barges.

'She's slipping back out of the slings.'

'Stop the capstan,' Michell shouted. 'Stop pumping.' Quick re-actions halted the movement before it got out of control. To prevent a recurrence the men hurriedly passed wires from the after capstans on the barges through the hawse-pipes on K13 and back to the capstans. Now they had wires looped through the hull itself. But Michell was not inclined to chance raising her again. And he could not use the torpedo tubes as an escape route: the lower lips still lay two inches under water. He called down the pipe to tell the entombed men that the plans had to be changed. Naturally they wanted to know why.

The news could not have come at a worse moment. First, the blocked pipe had upset them. Then, soon afterwards, someone caused a short circuit while connecting a lead to the starter of the compressor. The main fuse blew in the switchboard, throwing the submarine into darkness. An hour later the electricians contrived to get one light to work; otherwise, they had only three torches.

The angle of the boat frayed their tempers, too. She was inclined at sixteen degrees from the horizontal. Water and oil had spread over the linoleum which covered the decking, making it greasy. Men fell repeatedly, sliding down the one-in-six incline, knocking others down and striking themselves on projections before they stopped against a bulkhead. Professor Hillhouse, the naval architect, was standing near the forward end of the officers' quarters, holding on to a chain above his head, when his feet were knocked from under him by someone going aft involuntarily in a sitting position. He was left swinging on the chain.

Even little things made them edgy. The hissing from the air pipe annoyed them beyond reason. 'Take that bloody pipe away up forward,' they said, and 'Shove the damned thing aft.' Through the periscope they could see the ships gathered about the bows of the submarine and the men working on them; and they were irritated by the rate of progress. Surely the upper torpedo tubes were clear of the water now? In a moment of rashness they eased open a cover on one of the tubes. Water cascaded over them. They quickly screwed the cover down.

On the surface arguments once more developed about the rescue methods. Michell and Herbert wanted to cut a hole through the bows with an oxy-acetylene torch. Captain Young, the Naval Salvage Adviser, insisted that this was 'very bad salvage', and that they should continue trying to lift K13 till the torpedo tubes cleared the water. 'You can close the torpedo tubes if the need arises', he said, 'but you can't close a hole cut with the torch.' An executive from Fairfield's objected to using the oxy-acetylene flame because he was convinced that explosive gas had accumulated in the submarine. Captain Bartelott ended the arguments by authorising Michell to proceed. At this time a lorry brought to Shandon the rescue tube made during the night and morning by the draughtsmen, ironworkers and carpenters at the Fairfield yard. But there was no hope of using it.

Delay after delay now drove the men in K13 almost to despair. They spent a long time loosening stubborn nuts on a manhole cover only to hear the rescuers change their minds about the position at which they intended to cut through the hull. At two o'clock the chief engineer of *Thrush* at last applied the oxy-acetylene flame to the outer casing of the foremost compartment of the submarine. But only seconds later a fire broke out in the boat carrying the equipment and oxygen cylinders. The equipment was ruined. A fresh set had to be sought in Shandon.

In K13 a seaman said he could smell something strange. Was it chlorine? Everyone inhaled. Some thought they could smell it. Some laughed. How could there be chlorine, since no salt water had reached the batteries? But the seed of fear had been sown.

For some time Petty Officer Moth had stationed himself under the pipeline to pass messages to and from the surface. He had been telling Herbert something of the growing tension among the trapped men. Just after the fire Moth went to the wardroom lavatory, and while he was away he heard someone call up the pipe, 'We're getting chlorine gas, Captain.'

The effect of this message on the ships above was electric. If chlorine was building up the men would have to be out of K13 in thirty minutes or die. There was no time to wait for fresh oxy-acetylene gear. A chance had to be taken on lifting the bows and using the torpedo tubes as exits. The capstans and the barges were made ready.

Moth, furious with the rumour-monger, asked Professor Hillhouse, who had a torch, to go into the control-room with him and examine the batteries under the decking. They found no sign of sea-water. Moth hurried back to the pipeline.

'Captain', he called, 'there is no gas down here. We are all right. Please ignore the earlier message. One or two of the lads are just a bit jumpy, that's all.'

Herbert said, 'Thank God', and shouted to Michell to stop the lifting operation.

By three in the afternoon fresh oxy-acetylene gear arrived, and, with the water of the Gareloch lapping at his feet, the chief engineer from *Thrush* cut a hole roughly two feet square in the forecastle deck of K13. Between the outer hull and pressure hull was a free-flooding compartment which was lying largely below the surface of the loch, and was almost full of water. No pumps were available, so the men had to bale out the water with buckets. Herbert called down the pipeline that this would take about twenty minutes; then the engineer could cut through the pressure hull. In the bow torpedo-room, by the dim light of a torch, the men tore away the wood lining in the roof and clustered expectantly on and around the torpedo tubes.

Four flap valves operated by hand wheels inside the submarine controlled the entry of water through the sides of the free-flooding compartment. The rescue party assumed that these valves were closed. For an hour they laboriously baled out the compartment.

'When are you going to start cutting?' Hillhouse called up the voice-pipe.

'In about a quarter of an hour', Herbert replied. 'There's not much water left.'

The fifteen minutes dragged by.

'Have you started cutting yet?'

'No, not yet. Give us a few minutes more.'

In fact, the water-level in the compartment was not falling at all. Herbert suspected that the flap valves were jammed, and he had asked the engine department on *Thrush* to prepare a plastic material to block them. He checked with the men in K13 that the valves were closed, then told them reluctantly, 'I'm afraid it's taking longer than we expected to get the water out. The valves must be jammed open. We shall have to send a diver down to cover them.'

Above and below the water, the strain was unbearable. To the men in K13 it had seemed for three hours that rescue was only minutes away. Those on the salvage ships were tensed because the hole in the outer hull was barely six inches above the surface of the loch; and the tide was rising.

In the submarine Petty Officer Moth, who had learned in his naval career never to take anything for granted, went forward with McLean to examine the flap valve controls. One of the four wheels turned easily. The valve was, incredibly, partly open. As fast as the men above were baling the water out of the compartment, the Gareloch was flowing back through the valve. McLean locked the valve tight with a wheel spanner. Moth hurried aft to tell Herbert.

On one of the barges the crew had been rigging a suction pipe from their engine-room, and now, as the good news came from below, they passed it through the hole in the deck of K13. The water-level fell quickly, and in a few minutes the pressure hull lay bare. It was eight o'clock. The engineer lowered himself into the compartment and the acetylene torch was passed down to him.

In K13 the men sat or stood or crouched in total darkness. The torch batteries had given out. They talked in hushed tones. In the confined space they were glad once more to wave the hissing air pipe over their faces. Each was secretly confident that he would see the sky again; but each was reluctant to admit it to himself, let alone say it aloud.

A spot on the roof glowed red and the ghostly blue light of the oxy-acetylene flame burst through it, playing weirdly over the anxious, fascinated faces. As the roaring flame ate all too slowly through the thick steel, the prisoners, the rescuers and the people waiting on the shore willed the submarine not to move, the wires holding her not to break.

A shout went across the water from the deck of the submarine: 'The hole's cut.'

From the wardroom Lieutenant Singer, who had recovered his composure sufficiently to resume command, called out, 'Civilians first.'

The exodus began soon after nine o'clock. Only three inches now separated the edge of the hole from the loch; but the tide had stopped rising. It was a beautiful, calm night with a clear sky and a full moon. Arc lamps bathed the decks of the rescue ships and the absurdly tilted snout of K13 in brilliant light. On the submarine Herbert was among those standing by to help the men out. As the first head and shoulders appeared a tremendous cheer crossed the water and resounded against the far hillside. The same welcome greeted every man. Blinded by the fierce lights, they were shepherded from K13 across a gangway on to *Thrush.*

In his anxiety the engineer had cut the inner hole only 18 inches square, with the result that men of heavy build had to be dragged through it forcibly. Many left their coats behind. At the request of the salvage men Singer made certain that all the watertight doors forward of the beam torpedo-room were closed. Professor Hillhouse and William Wallace, the representative of the Edinburgh boiler firm, helped him. In accordance with regulations, the lieutenant was the last of the 46 men to leave. He did so shortly after ten o'clock, nearly 57 hours after K13 had gone down.

Motor-boats sped the men ashore. Though all were in varying stages of exhaustion, they could walk unaided. Nevertheless, many people from the crowd on the shore insisted on taking them by the arms and supporting and guiding them to the Shandon hotel. There they were properly received with hot baths and lavish suppers. The telephone was in great demand among all the civilians, excepting Captain Duncan, the Clyde pilot, who merely settled down quietly in front of the lounge fire to read a newspaper. When chaffed about his calmness he excused himself by saying that he had missed three days' news.

Out on the Gareloch Michell and his crew wearily disconnected their air leads from K13 and moved E50 out of the way of the salvage ships. As they let go E50's anchor they were almost asleep on their feet. Since leaving John Brown's yard early on the Monday morning, they had worked without rest for more than sixty hours. To them, undoubtedly, the 47 survivors from K13 owed their lives.

The next day rescuers and rescued received a congratulatory telegram from King George V. The civilians returned to their homes; Moth took the crew to the billets in Glasgow; E50 sailed back to her makers' yard; and Herbert and Singer remained at Shandon to await the salvaging of K13. Using additional lifting wires and blowing compressed air down the two pipelines, Captain Young strove through the day to hold the bows of the submarine above the surface as a first step in raising her. But on the morning tide her weight increased so much that he had to slacken the purchases from *Thrush* and the trawler. Water was obviously leaking through the forward bulkheads. At six that evening she tore the bollards out of the barges and sank.

Before the operation began again the next morning the divers searched the bridge structure and found Goodhart's body trapped under the roof of the wheelhouse. He had either struck his head on the roof and lost consciousness, or drowned while trying to find a way out. The tin cylinder was still tucked under his belt.

On 19 February an Admiralty Court of Inquiry met in the board-room of the Fairfield company in Glasgow to consider the cause of the accident. The court consisted of Acting Captain Godfrey Corbett, the president; Commander Aubrey T. Tillard, of H.M.S. *Firedrake*; and Commander Ferdinand E.B. Fielman, the new captain of K14. Commodore (Submarines) Sydney Hall acted as the Admiralty's adviser. It was reported that the divers had found that the four 37-inch ventilators over the boiler-room had been left open, and that the indicators in the boiler-room stood at 'Open'. To the court's conster-nation, they had also found the engine-room hatch undone. Skinner, the electrical manager at Fairfield's, confirmed that all the ventilators had worked properly before K13 left the yard that Monday morning. Searle, the Admiralty ship overseer, said that on the Sunday he had tested every valve in the boat not once but several times, putting them under a pressure of 2,000 pounds. Herbert told the court that he had exercised the crew at diving stations daily for some three weeks and that Engineer-Lieutenant Lane had instructions to close all the open-ings before signalling to the control-room that the engine and boiler rooms were shut.

Lane's naval record was now put before the court. Over the previous seven years his commanding officers had consistently found his work and conduct exemplary: there were frequent references to his zeal, reliability, moderation and good judgment. Unable to offer an expla-nation for his lapse, the court decided that 'Engineer-Lieutenant Lane was solely responsible for the accident'.

It added: 'We consider that Lieutenant-Commander Herbert was fully justified in believing that the submarine was all shut off for diving, but we would suggest that as a check on the electrical indicator it would seem desirable to make use of the voice-pipe also.'

A conference called at the Admiralty in London by the Third Sea Lord considered the evidence, and authorised new safeguards for submarines in general, and K boats in particular. In the K class the indicators in the control-room were to be modified to operate directly from the engine-room and boiler-room openings, not through the hands of the engine-room staff. The number of civilians to be carried on future trials was to be strictly regulated. And no more submarines were to be numbered 13.

> A check on the human element has also been instituted, [Commodore Hall reported to the Sea Lords] by having a sentry in the boiler-room passage who can see through the bull's-eye window if they [the ventilators] are shut, as well as the man in the boiler-room itself.
>
> Whatever our mechanical contrivances or interlocking arrangements may be, there must always come a time in these vessels when safety depends on the perfect working of the human machine, a time when failures, perhaps only for an instant, of alertness or caution will bring disaster.
>
> The evidence is clear that some such failure occurred in the engine-room on this occasion under circumstances almost inconceivable as there was no hurry and the officer primarily concerned was the one who had requested that the vessel should dive in order to test these openings, with the condition of which he must have been fully acquainted.
>
> This is the first time we have had engineer officers in submarines, and the only possible explanation I can offer is that, probably due to very short experience, he had not his underwater sense of caution fully developed.
>
> It is hoped some recognition be made of those whom the court recommended – they did very well.

In fact, the authorities were sparing in their rewards. For his part, Fred Searle, who took over from Singer, was promoted to an Established Assistant Constructor, a position he had failed to achieve by examination after a three-year course at the Royal Naval College, Greenwich. McLean, Skinner and Bullen, of the Fairfield company, and Lake, the Peterborough youth, received 'an expression of appreciation' from the Lords Commissioners of the Admiralty. Michell and his crew were commended for 'working with the greatest zeal for forty-eight hours without rest'. Commander Goodhart received the posthumous award of the Albert Medal for gallantry in saving life at sea. Herbert got nothing. Singer did well for himself. At his death in Greenwich, Connecticut, in December 1953, *The Times* reported:

> His conduct in sustaining the morale of the crew of K13 until rescuers arrived, and in directing the work of rescue brought him appointment as flag lieutenant to the Commander-in-Chief at Portsmouth. Later, he was a planner of the Zeebrugge raid.

Up in the Gareloch, Captain Young's salvage party closed all the openings in the inner hull of K13 and fitted to each compartment an air-supply pipe and a water-discharge pipe. With these the water was gradually driven out of the boat, and six weeks after the accident, on 15 March, she bobbed to the surface as unexpectedly as she had gone down. During the afternoon of that day and the morning of the next, the bodies of the men drowned in the after half were removed. One clung to a ladder in the act of escape. In another's pocket was a wad of thirteen pound-notes, all but two of which were dry. Thirty-one coffins had naturally been prepared for the funeral that afternoon, but only twenty-nine bodies were laid out in front of the garage at Sandon Hydro. At last the mystery of the open hatch over the engine-room was solved; at last credence was given to the story of Annie McIntyre, the housemaid who claimed to have seen two men drown in the loch immediately after K13's dive. Those missing were Lane and John Steel, the foreman in the Fairfield engine department. As the sea had flooded into the engine-room, they had evidently opened the hatch when the air-pressure inside had equalled the water-pressure outside. They had managed to reach the surface only to succumb to the sudden reduction of pressure in their lungs. Strong underwater currents setting out of the Gareloch would have carried the men far down the estuary. Dragging operations now would be futile. John Steel was never found, but Lane's body was recovered on a distant bank of the Clyde some two months later, and was buried with the other victims in the little graveyard at Faslane Bay, which overlooks the scene of the tragedy.

Ten bodies of the naval stokers in the crew could not positively be identified, and their headstones bear the inscription KNOWN TO BE BURIED IN THIS PLOT. In the centre of the plot the ship's company of H.M. Submarine Depot, Fort Blockhouse, Gosport, later erected a memorial stone. In Elder Park, opposite the Fairfield works in Glasgow, the management and employees of the firm similarly built a drinking fountain in honour of the dead. The inscription on the fountain credited Commander Goodhart with the Victoria Cross. No one has ever corrected the error.

On 16 March a tug towed the muddy, forlorn K13 back up the Clyde to the Fairfield yard for a refit. The firm completed the sister ship, K14, but never built another submarine.

From the hydraulic system of K13 the shipwrights recovered William Wallace's two-shilling piece, dented by the water-pressure, and the firm returned it to him with their compliments. Wallace put the coin in his pocket and almost spent it, then had it set in a framed photograph of K13. For a week after the accident he could not sleep, but otherwise he suffered no ill-effects until several years later, when he developed deafness. Three years after the accident the same complaint brought about the premature discharge from the Navy of Leading Signalman Arthur Riley.

None of the officers and a few of the civilians who survived from K13 ever boarded a submarine again. Herbert took command of a flotilla of four anti-submarine trawlers at Falmouth. Lieutenant Rideal also went back to surface ships. And Singer got his staff appointment.

Of the rest of the crew almost nothing is known, except that they had to report at Fort Blockhouse after ten days' leave. Only one of them, Chief Petty Officer Oscar Moth, had not done with K13. Moth suffered the most astonishing after-effects from the accident: within a few weeks he lost every hair on his head. But this did not deter him when he received his new posting to K22, alias the refitted K13.

CHAPTER FOUR

K FOR CALAMITY

I never met anybody who had the least affection for the K class and they were looked on with fear and loathing. After all, they murdered many of their officers and crews. – Commander George F. Bradshaw, D.S.O. R.N. (retd.), 1959.

I think the antipathy towards K boats was universal among most officers and men. – Commander R.J. Brooke-Booth, D.S.C., R.N. (retd.), 1959.

My dad's name is F.F. Hills and he was a stoker first class. He joined K10 at Barrow-in-Furness in 1917 . . . He hopes they never build any more like them for poor men to live in as they made more men sick than any other boat. – Mrs A.I. Hammond, of Barr

During 1917 the people responsible at the Admiralty for the production of K boats practised to an astonishing degree the habits of self-deception and of making excuses. The Navy, public funds, seven shipyards and, most important, a number of high reputations in Whitehall and Scapa Flow were irrevocably committed to the new submarines. It was unthinkable, therefore, that they should fail. Yet all thirteen of the K boats which underwent trials between January and May 1917 ran into trouble.

No one at the Admiralty cared to consider the mishaps jointly, or, at this stage, to reassess the seaworthiness of the new class. After all, the accidents were easily explained. Human error had sunk K13, and inexperience had caused K3 to bury her bows in the sea-bed in Stokes Bay and to flood her boilers in the North Sea. A designer would expect an untried vessel to develop idiosyncrasies: it would be a simple matter to advise captains how to deal with them.

But few parts of the submarine seemed free from fault during the trials. K1 developed so many faults that her trials lasted from January to May. K2, built alongside K1 at the naval dockyard at Portsmouth, suffered an explosion and fire on her first diving trials. The insulation broke down in her electric motors. In the instant before the fuses blew a sheet of flame flashed across the engine-room, setting alight planks and oily waste left by the dockyard workers. With no fire extinguishers on board, the captain, Commander Noel Laurence, surfaced the submarine, and the crew put out the fire with buckets of water passed down the engine-room hatch.

At the end of January K2 went on her acceptance trials. That day the sea was choppy and the temperature freezing. Ice was forming on the shore. Soon after the submarine cleared the harbour, water began to slop into the casing beneath the funnels and through the mushroom shaped ventilators into the boiler-room. In Stokes Bay the hooters blew to signal diving stations, and the vents opened to flood the main ballast tanks. In the engine-room an E.R.A. threw the lever to close the boiler-room vents; but the electrical indicator did not light up. The engineer officer, Alexander Mark-Wardlaw, shouted down the voice-pipe to the control-room: 'Surface immediately!' The call came in time. Mark-Wardlaw examined the vents and concluded that the icy sea-water had partly solidified the oil in the hydraulic system. Wax must have settled out of the oil, jamming the actuating cylinders. Back in harbour, as he took a sample of the oil to the Admiralty chemist to test his theory, news came through of the sinking of K13 in the Gareloch. The chemist confirmed that the oil from K2 was a type which became wax-bound at around 30°F. An instruction immediately went out to all K boats to use only Arctic non-freezing oil in their hydraulic systems.

Farther down the south coast, at the naval dockyard at Devonport, K6 and K7 fared no better than their sister ships. On her first submergence in a non-tidal basin in the North Dockyard, K6 refused to surface. Many dockyard workers and naval personnel were on board. The inspector of engine-fitters at the yard, a man named Selley, traced the fault to the compressed-air system and temporarily repaired it. After two hours of anxiety, the submarine rose to the surface. By now she inspired so much awe in the yard that a number of workmen refused to dive in her a second time. Selley collected a scratch crew of civilians for the next submergence in the basin. This time K6 performed obediently, and the dockyard mutineers regained their confidence. The incident was hushed up, and few people outside the dockyard knew what lay behind a small news item which appeared in the *Naval and Military Record* two years later, on 23 April, 1919. It stated simply: 'The Lord Lieutenant of Devon presented to L. Selley the silver medal of the Order of the British Empire for courage and devotion to duty "on the occasion of the trial of a new submarine".'

Meanwhile, K4, following K3 out of the Barrow yard of Messrs

Vickers, went aground during her trials. She was refloated. On the Clyde the Fairfield yard completed K14, and she followed the path of her sister, K13, into the Gareloch for diving trials. All went well until she sprang a leak one night while at anchor in the loch. A rating named Arthur Hime was testing the specific gravity of the batteries when he found the compartment under the officers' quarters full of water. The plating over B ballast tank had worked loose. No one had noticed that chlorine gas was filling the submarine. Like her ill-fated sister, she had to return to the shipyard towed by a tug.

Leaky plates, faulty electrical insulation, frozen oil; these, it was argued, were incidental flaws which could occur on any new ship. They could be lethal, but once detected they were easily put right. More serious defects, however, became apparent as the submarines scraped through their trials and steamed north in ones and twos to join the Grand Fleet at Scapa Flow. These were defects inherent in the design and therefore common to the entire class.

Among perceptive submariners the very seaworthiness of the boats had been under suspicion from the start. When rough seas had shattered the windows in the bridge of K3 on her trials an Admiralty overseer had recommended the use of thicker glass. But now it was obvious that this did not begin to solve the problem. The bows of the boats lacked lifting buoyancy. At 12 knots or more, even in the most moderate of sea-ways, the bows would not rise. They sliced through the waves, throwing torrents of water over the foredeck, bridge and superstructure. In a heavy sea a K boat had to reduce speed, heave to or dive. The large, flat surface of the foredeck gave the submarine an alarming tendency to dive. Many a time an officer of the watch lightened the ballast in the bows to make doubly sure that his submarine would not suddenly slide under water. In these conditions it was impossible for the submarine to keep station with the Fleet, let alone take up a tactical position. It was impossible, too, for her men to man the forward gun: most of the time it was half submerged. Trying to fire the deck torpedo tubes was almost as futile because water seeped into them and damaged the torpedoes.

For the men behind the canvas screen which served as a bridge the work of conning the ship was uncomfortable and at times dangerous. It was equally unpleasant below. The great length and narrow beam made the boat pitch and roll unpleasantly, to no set rhythm. Water tumbling down the conning-tower hatch would splash off the control room floor, earthing the switchboards and shocking anyone who gripped the conning-tower ladder. In the boiler-room the stokers wore oilskins as a protection from the water pouring through the ventilators.

Sometimes a wave would find its way down the funnels, the boilers would flash back and another stoker would lack eyebrows. One night the ventilator fans in K2 scattered incoming water with such force that it broke the glass gauges showing the water-levels in the boilers. Even the engine-room was not immune: the bigger waves would roll well aft over the ventilation intake and shower on to the men on the control platform. K11 had hardly left the Armstrong Whitworth yard on the Tyne before she was back at Cammell Laird's at Birkenhead to have her generator replaced. Salt water had wrecked it.

The K boat was as vulnerable to heavy seas from the stern as from the bows. When running in rough conditions with a quartering sea, or with the sea right aft, she was easily pooped. One day four K boats were returning through the Pentland Firth to Scapa from exercises in the North Sea. They were steaming at 10 knots in line ahead formation behind a light cruiser, the flagship of the Commodore (Submarines). The Pentland Firth is a notorious spot when wind and tide conflict. On this day a gale was blowing in from the North Sea, and waves twenty feet high were building up. On K2 the officer of the watch realised that the rollers were overtaking the submarine and rearing menacingly over her stern. Ignoring the flagship's earlier orders and the possibility of a court-martial, he ordered the engine-room to increase speed to 20 knots. The submarine surged past the flagship and sailed safely into the harbour. Her three sister ships, meanwhile, disappeared in clouds of smoke and steam as water filled their boiler-rooms and forced them to dive. Once under water, they could not compete with the ebbing, 7½-knot tide. They had to retreat and wait out the storm in bays along the Scottish coast. K2's officer of the watch was not court-martialled.

If the seaworthiness of the K boat on the surface was questionable, her diving characteristics were positively alarming. It became clear that K3's nose-dive was no freak occurrence. The K boat's great length gave her a large moment of inertia, like that of a giant seesaw. When she began to swing her bows down she was far more difficult to straighten than a submarine of normal length. If the diving angle became too steep, the flat, broad areas of the upper deck and of the superstructure tended to act as an extra hydroplane, increasing the downward thrust and making correction still more difficult and sometimes impossible. At some time in their careers most, if not all, of the class nose-dived out of control on to the sea-bed.

Before a dive a K boat had to be trimmed with great care, making accurate allowance for the changes caused by variations in the density of the seawater and by the consumption of fuel, water, ammunition and stores. Fully submerged, the submarine displaced more than 2,500 tons. If she were trimmed too heavily, or heavy in the bows, the two sets of hydroplanes and the arrangements for blowing the ballast tanks could not be relied upon to correct her. Because of this, and because the boats would not withstand the pressure below a depth of 150 feet, the captains were always most cautious about choosing a spot to dive.

The method of carrying fuel caused another hazard. The undersides of the fuel tanks were open to the sea, so that the oil actually floated on the water and was drawn by pumps from the tops of the tanks. As the submarine used the oil its place was taken by seawater. This self-compensating system kept the weight of the submarine reasonably constant and eased the problem of adjusting the ballast. Under stable conditions it worked well; but if the boat rolled severely the oil and water tended to emulsify, and this mixture put out the boiler fires. The phenomenon was called losing suction. It happened to K9 on her maiden voyage from Barrow-in-Furness to Scapa. It happened to many other K boats, too.

Now and again the K boats at Scapa Flow took part in exercises in the harbour with units of the Grand Fleet. On the day before one such mock attack the first lieutenant of K2 went to bed early feeling unwell and left the trimming of the main ballast to the care of another officer who had recently arrived on board. The job involved adjusting the weight of the boat with ballast water, so that on flooding the external main ballast tanks she would have neutral buoyancy: that is, be equal to the weight of the water she displaced. In this state she would balance in the water rather than float and would dive or surface simply by movements of the hydroplanes. In smaller submarines in which the new officer had previously served it was a common practice to have the trim slightly heavy for speedier diving.

The newcomer trimmed K2 in this manner. The next morning the captain positioned the submarine for an attack fine on the bows of the flagship of the 8th Battle Squadron: then he flooded the externals and dived. She went down far too fast. She would not answer to the hydroplanes, and blowing the auxiliary tanks did not check her. The depth gauge showed 100 feet and she began to strain and creak. The captain knew that the water thereabouts was 360 feet deep, but at only half that depth the pressure would crush the submarine. Danger lay above, too, in the shape of the hulls of the battle-cruisers. Taking the better of the two chances, the first lieutenant leaped to the master compressed-air valve and emptied all the external tanks. K2 groaned, straightened, stood still. Slowly she began to rise. As her rate of ascent increased the crew tensed themselves, anticipating a collision. But nothing happened. She bobbed safely to the surface. At the earliest opportunity the new officer received a short course from his colleagues in the delicate art of trimming a K boat.

The submariner regards the crash-dive as a basic tactical weapon: but a crash-dive was beyond the K class. On average it took five minutes to shut off the boilers, retract the funnels, close the ventilators and hatches, evacuate the boiler-room, fill the ballast tanks and submerge. The fastest recorded time was 3 minutes 25 seconds by K8. During the diving procedure several of the captains found time to leave the bridge and walk along the superstructure, not for a last-minute constitutional but to ensure that all the holes were closed. The funnels fitted tightly into the wells, and the smallest piece of flotsam could, and did, prevent the funnels or the ventilators from closing properly. The result, if the blockage went undetected, was a set of blown fuses in the funnel motor or, worse, a flooded boiler-room.

For those in the boiler-room diving was a nightmarish ordeal. The stokers worked in a room so small that they could not step back more than a few feet from the furnaces. The heat, the roaring of the induction fans forcing air into the furnaces, the pumps thumping, the smell of hot fuel and oil turned the place into a miniature inferno. At the sound of the diving hooter the stokers rushed to shut off the fuel and stop the fans and pumps. As the noise died the heat rose. Finally, one man climbed a ladder to shut off the stop valves above the boilers. If his captain was wise the man inspected the ventilators, too. Then, often in a state of collapse from the heat, he staggered through the twin doors of the airlock which led into the engine-room.

Complications could arise while diving. The boiler-room could catch fire. On a North Sea patrol K11 made an emergency dive when an unidentified ship came over the horizon. In the boiler-room the stokers could not turn off the fuel pump. Oil flooding the compartment caught fire, and, enemy ship or no, K11 was forced to surface. By the time the fire was out it had wrecked the boiler-room and melted all the electric cables passing through it. By this time, too, the unknown ship had disappeared. Unable to dive and practically helpless, the submarine began a long crawl back home using her diesel engine and electric motors. Fortunately, she went unmolested. Near the Scottish coast a patrolling destroyer took her in tow, and once more in her first year afloat she found herself in dry dock for a refit.

The same submarine suffered from another fault which hampered the diving and underwater performance of several boats in the class. At depths of more than 80 feet her forward hydroplanes jammed. In other boats the after hydroplanes, sometimes called the diving rudders, gave trouble. One theory had it that the guide rods in the control gear were not strong enough. Another blamed the fault on an inherent weakness in the stern, which was oval-shaped in section. The theorists reckoned that this shape, 'like a duck's arse', would more readily distort under pressure, with the result that the bearings in the control gear jammed. Whatever the cause, it was the least pleasant of discoveries when, with the submarine forging downwards, the hydroplane wheels refused to turn.

In spite of their size, the K boats did not offer greater all-round comfort than the conventional submarines. The officers were certainly better off. The captain had a small cabin; each officer had a comfortable bunk; and the ward-room was relatively spacious and well-furnished. They even had a four-foot bath with fresh water heated by steam or electricity. But in the stern half of the boat where most of the men had their quarters the accommodation was not so good. The petty officers and the engine-room artificers had separate curtained messes, but they were cramped. The heat from the boilers pervaded the ship. The additional and larger fans fitted in the boiler-rooms after the early experience in K3 made little difference to the temperature. Long after diving the residual heat from the boilers kept the submarine like 'an unventilated oven', 'an underwater hell'. In the engine-room, where each bunk was shared by three men, and on the mess decks, it was commonplace to find pools of condensation under the bunks. The ventilation was so poor that the diesel engine was often started to draw fresh air into the after end of the boat. To make conditions worse, some of the self-compensating fuel tanks lay under the mess decks and under the engine-room. The tank tops were the mess floors, and the seams were rarely oil-tight. During a dive the pressure in the tanks was the pressure obtained from the depth of the dive. Frequently oil seeped through the seams on to the deck floors and swilled underfoot.

Even in harbour the K boat man could not escape his discomforts. Unlike other submarines, the class was not provided with depot ships, in which the crews could enjoy a respite from their cramped quarters. The navy classified the K boat as a self-contained warship. The tedium of life in harbour and the crew's pent-up energy led to frequent squabbles and fist-fights. For light relief the captain of K6, Geoffrey Layton, initiated a small garden for his men on the peaty shore near the submarine's mooring at Scapa. The rabbits ate at least half of the produce, but the garden gave the men exercise, an interest and fresh vegetables in harbour.

It was hardly surprising that the Grand Fleet did not receive its full complement of K boats as early in 1917 as the flag officers expected. Equally it was not surprising that the two flotillas into which the boats were formed were rarely up to their full strength, particularly during that year. But when King George V visited the Grand Fleet in the summer of 1917 a K boat was thought worthy of his inspection. K1 was selected for the honour. After the visit the King was photographed leaving the submarine up a step-ladder. The funnels were purposely retracted. The photograph would receive widespread publication, and the Admiralty still saw K boats very much as a secret and surprise weapon. In the mind of the enemy, funnels on a submarine would signify speed, and speed would indicate fleet submarines; and that would give the whole game away.

Another distinguished visitor to Scapa Flow at that time was the journalist, politician and financier Horatio Bottomley, then at the height of his popularity. He went on board K6 and found that the crew had bedecked their quarters with copies of *John Bull*, the magazine he founded. They fêted him. He in return promised them extra leave; but, of course, they never got it.

As 1917 progressed it became maddeningly clear to the flag officers of the Grand Fleet that the German High Seas Fleet had no intention of doing battle. It became clear, too, that the Germans had not yet equipped themselves with fleet submarines. But at least the Grand Fleet now had a class of warships which the enemy did not have: what matter if the end for which they were conceived was not materialising? Surely they could be put to some other use?

During the summer when they were not engaged on hazardous fleet exercises, they were assigned to anti-submarine patrols in the North Sea. Anti-submarine craft require manoeuvrability, a quality in which the K boat did not excel. A submarine hunting U-boats also needed the ability to crash-dive in half a minute, not five, and to make a quick getaway on surfacing, not spend fifteen to twenty minutes raising a head of steam and belching clouds of black diesel smoke in the process.

The anti-submarine patrols by K boats bordered often on the farcical and once or twice on the tragic. Between 15 and 24 June the 12th Submarine Flotilla, then consisting of K1, K2, K4, K6, K7 and K8, took part in a large concerted anti-U-boat sweep by the destroyers and submarines of the Grand Fleet. Naval Intelligence advised Admiral Beatty, the commander-in-chief, that a number of U-boats would pass north through the North Sea between those dates. The short nights gave a favourable opportunity for anti-submarine operations, and on 13 June Beatty issued orders for Operation B.B. The object was 'to force enemy submarines to dive through certain areas occupied by destroyers, so that they would be on the surface while passing through adjacent areas occupied by our submarines'.

The total force of 4 flotilla leaders, 49 destroyers and 17 submarines was divided into nine groups covering an area which extended roughly round the northern half of Scotland. During the ten days of the operation the force sighted U-boats 37 times, made 11 attacks on them, but sank none. The U-boats, meanwhile, disposed of one British armed trawler, and three Danish, three British and two Norwegian merchantmen. K7 distinguished herself. On 16 June at 11 a.m., as she began a diving patrol in her area, the Fair Isle Channel, other ships in the force identified her as a U-boat. The destroyers *Observer* and *Rocket* gave chase. The captain of K7, Lieutenant-Commander Gilbert Kellett, dodged the destroyers and their depth-charges, and then he surfaced and quickly signalled that he was on their side. At 3.12 p.m., back under water again, Kellett sighted a U-boat steering south. Nine minutes later he got within range and fired a torpedo from one of the beam tubes. It missed. At 3.29 Kellett fired all four bow tubes at the submarine. The entire salvo ran on the surface, but the U-boat could not avoid the third torpedo. It struck her amidships. Incredibly, nothing happened. The U-boat merely altered course and opened fire on K7, which had surfaced. Kellett retaliated with one more torpedo from a starboard tube, but again missed the target. At this point, with the steam submarine overhauling him, the German captain dived to safety. Naval Intelligence later confirmed that the U-boat, U95, was returning to base; that K7's torpedo struck her under the conning-tower; and that it failed to explode.

During Operation B.B. K2 worked in the same area as K7. One morning the Fair Isle lighthouse-keepers reported to Scapa Flow that they had seen K2 strike a mine and sink with all hands. Appropriate telegrams went out to the next of kin. In the early hours two mornings later lookouts on the Grand Fleet in Scapa Flow reported that an unidentified submarine was entering the harbour. Pandemonium reigned until the submarine revealed her identity. She was K2. What had happened near the lighthouse was that, in hazy conditions, the submarine had made a test firing of her 4-inch gun immediately before starting her diving patrol. At a safe range the gun crew had aimed at the lighthouse, and when the shell exploded on the water it appeared to the lighthouse-keepers that the submarine had struck a mine. The next moment, when she slid underwater, they were convinced she had sunk.

Another incident during the same operation concerned K1. The captain of K4, Commander David Stocks, found a convenient anchorage near Bow Rock, in the Orkneys, where he could lie in wait for U-boats returning through the Fair Isle Channel. He mentioned the spot to the captain of K1, Commander Charles Stewart Benning. On her next patrol K1 tried to make use of the anchorage but ran aground. Her batteries had to be removed before she floated free. Benning told a court-martial later that the rats in his boat had eaten the relevant part of his chart. He got away with it.

Admiral Beatty announced that he regarded Operation B.B. as 'on the whole successful in arresting a serious enemy submarine attack', and throughout the autumn and early part of the winter the K boats took part in further anti-submarine patrols. From time to time they assumed their real function as fleet submarines and accompanied sections of the Grand Fleet in sweeps along the enemy coastline. The operations were designed to tempt the High Seas Fleet out to fight. The 12th Submarine Flotilla accompanied part of the fleet on one such sweep which began on 16 November, 1917. The K boats saw no action, but at about eight o'clock on the night of the 17th two of them collided off the Danish coast. The flotilla and its surface leader, *Blonde*, were changing course at the time. K4 ran down K1, crippling her. *Blonde* took off the crew and tried to tow the submarine, but worsening weather and seas defeated her. The captain of the flotilla leader decided that he was too close to the enemy coast to await better conditions, so at about 10 p.m. he sank K1 with gunfire.

The accident confirmed the view of many submariners that submarines worked better and more safely on their own. In line ahead formation at night the men on watch on a K boat had great difficulty keeping station behind the dim light showing on the submarine ahead. The submarines had such a low freeboard that the light would often disappear behind the waves.

About the time of the loss of K1 news came that the class was to undergo structural alterations. One at a time the boats were to be fitted with false bows, a huge, bulbous, free-flooding structure which spoiled the sleek lines of the hull but was designed to improve its seaworthiness. They were known as swan bows. Other changes were to be made: one gun and the deck torpedo tubes were to be removed; the two remaining guns were to be positioned on the superstructure; on some boats a permanent brass bridge screen was to replace the folding canvas contraption; depth-charge throwers were to be fitted; and, arising from Commander Goodhart's death in K13, the flap hatch in the wheelhouse roof was to be positioned immediately above the conning-tower hatch.

The crews regarded these changes with mixed feelings. They were pleased that the boats were being improved, but dismayed at what amounted to an official admission of their unseaworthiness.

In all the unsettling circumstances tension grew among some crews and they resorted to hard drinking. On K2 the loss overboard of a stoker while on sea-watch one night in Scapa Flow harbour brought the men close to breaking-point. One Sunday they refused to go ashore to church, at that time a compulsory duty. They said they would not pray by order, only by inclination. A reading of the penalties for disobeying a command, leavened by some appreciation of their fears and discomforts, changed their minds by the following Sunday.

When the crew of a J-class submarine heard in September 1917 that some of the men might be drafted to the refitted K13, now numbered K22, several of them fell mysteriously ill. This and other methods used to avoid the draft proved unnecessary so far as that particular boat was concerned. Nevertheless, there were fifty other submariners who that month found themselves travelling compulsorily to Glasgow to join K22. During the rebuilding she had received the nickname 'Newhaven Packet', and the distinction of being painted in oils by Charles Pears. Her new captain was Lieutenant-Commander Charles de Burgh, D.S.O., her coxswain Oscar Moth.

The programme of trials began at the beginning of October. De Burgh's wife had moved into the Shandon Hydropathic Hotel to be near her husband, and, with all the local people aware that K13 was returning to the Gareloch, she overheard much gloomy gossip. 'It was tempting providence to rebuild that submarine.' 'It's murder sending a crew to sea in a boat like that.' On the day of the first diving trial in the loch a crowd gathered on the lochside. On K22 de Burgh asked Moth to point out exactly the spot where K13 had gone down. De Burgh dived her in the same position. On shore Mrs de Burgh saw horror on every face. 'That's exactly where she sank last time.' A thousand breaths were held as K22's periscopes went under water, reappeared, then submerged again. Ten minutes later she surfaced and the trial was over. Two weeks later a four-hour acceptance trial proved entirely satisfactory, and at long last the Navy took possession of the submarine. Simultaneously in London a conclusion was reached in arguments concerning the award of salvage money to the naval vessels which had raised K13. The Admiralty's senior legal adviser decreed that 'as the vessel was sunk . . . through a mistake of a naval officer . . . a salvage claim for profit to the

Crown would be inappropriate and a claim for expenses only should suffice.'

In mid-October K22 sailed from the Clyde to join a newly forming flotilla of K boats at Rosyth, on the Firth of Forth. The flotilla was numbered 13.

CHAPTER FIVE

THE BATTLE OF MAY ISLAND

The K class . . . have been successful vessels . . . In fleet exercises they always fulfilled the functions for which they were designated. – Submarine Administration, Training and Construction, published by the Technical History Section of the Admiralty, 1921.

The only good thing about K boats was that they never engaged the enemy. – Rear-Admiral Ernest W. Leir, R.N. (retd.), in an interview, February 1961.

In December of 1917 Vice-Admiral Beatty moved his K boats from Scapa Flow to Rosyth, believing that they would be better placed tactically in the Forth estuary. About this time several of the boats received new officers. Some were transferred within the flotillas: the rest came from other classes of submarines. One boat, K6, took on a seventeen-year-old midshipman to do his two months' small-ship training. He was Lord Louis Francis Albert Victor Nicholas Mountbatten.

Before the move from Scapa Flow a new captain took over K7. A wiry, boyish lieutenant-commander named Samuel Maryon Gorton Gravener replaced Commander Kellett, the man who had hit a U-boat with a dud torpedo. Gravener received his new appointment while on leave after captaining an E-class submarine in the Mediterranean. Knowing nothing of the reputation which K boats were making for themselves, he left for Scapa feeling pleased at being given command of one of the Navy's biggest and fastest submarines.

Gravener had been in the Submarine Service ever since he had left the Royal Naval College at Greenwich as a sub-lieutenant in 1908. When volunteers were called for he had put his name forward for the unlikeliest of reasons: the extra pay enabled him to indulge in his favourite sports, riding and hunting.

When he arrived on K7 the officers were giving a party. Whisky bottles and glasses hid the wardroom table. The party was in honour of no special occasion, and there was something about the atmosphere which perturbed the new captain. After a night or two he found that on more than one of the K boats life in harbour was a constant round of drinking. The first time he was taken out in K7 he was astounded at the demeanour of the crew when they went to diving-stations. He swore afterwards that the coxswain's knees were trembling as he sat at the hydroplane controls. When Gravener assumed full command he determined to try to boost the men's confidence. At his first dive he allowed the submarine to go only a foot or two under water before bringing her sharply to the surface. He wanted to show that he knew how to handle the boat, that she would do what he wanted. The surprise gesture immediately had a good effect on crew morale.

What Gravener had not known about K boats before his arrival he soon learned from his fellow-officers, from experience, and from observation. Within a day or two of the move to Rosyth he saw a classic example of their wayward behaviour. Returning to base from a practice run and some target-shooting in the estuary, he came across the stern of a K boat waggling out of the water at an angle of about thirty degrees, with its propellers threshing the air. The bows were stuck in the mud bottom of the Forth. While Gravener pondered what to do, the submarine blew its ballast tanks, extricated itself and surfaced. It took barely a month for Gravener to revise completely his attitude to his new command. By then the only good thing about it was that he was able to lodge his wife close by the naval base. In common with the wives of many officers at Rosyth, she stayed at the Hawse Inn, a name which was popularly misrepresented by almost every sailor on the base.

By now the K flotillas boasted several of the most renowned captains in the Submarine Service. The 12th Flotilla, led by the light cruiser *Fearless*, was commanded by Captain Charles James Colebrook Little, who had captained one of the Navy's first operational submarines. His counterpart in the 13th Flotilla, on the light cruiser *Ithuriel*, was Commander Leir, who earlier in the war had been an intrepid E boat captain, and had commanded the first K boat, K3. In K2 was Laurence, who had broken through the German minefields into the Baltic early in the war; in K6 was Layton, who had also run the Baltic gauntlet and had returned home to take command of the Navy's first steam submarine, that experimental flop *Swordfish*; in K14 was Harbottle, who had gone spy-catching along the coast of Crete in an E class submarine disguised as a U-boat; there was Dobson in K10, who had sunk a

U-boat when it fell into the trap of attacking a trawler which was towing his C boat underwater; K4 had Stocks, who had dived an E boat through the Dardanelles and plundered Turkish shipping in the Sea of Marmara; K8 was commanded by Ross-Turner, whose E boat had taken on the German Fleet single-handed off Borkum; there was Shove in K3, who kept a pet white rat in his monkey jacket, Hutchings in K5, Layard in K9, Calvert in K11, Bower in K12, Hearn in K17, and de Burgh and Gravener in K22 and K7. They were all men who relished action, who had distinguished themselves hunting the enemy on their own or at the most in packs of two or three submarines. Now, cooped up with the Grand Fleet at Rosyth, they were seeing no action, only abortive patrols and sweeps. They had lost their independence and some of the spirit that went with it. The 'greatest submarines a navy ever built' were turning into white elephants of the sea, charging hither and thither, doing all the wrong things. And no one would admit it.

After the Christmas and New Year festivities, which briefly eased the tension in the K flotillas, K9 left Rosyth for Chatham dockyard to be fitted with her swan bows. The cruiser *Southampton* accompanied her. K9 was noted for a motto derived from a ponderous pun. The wooden plaque in her control-room carried the one word GARM, which was the name of the dog of the underworld in Norse mythology, and of a real-life dog owned by King George V. Thus K9's motto was a ca-nine. The crew of the submarine felt pleased at the prospect of spending an idle month on the outskirts of London. In normal conditions it would have taken them only two days to reach Chatham, but off the Northumberland coast K9 ran into heavy weather. While changing course she was pooped by a sea which poured down her funnels and put out her boiler fires. Next, the captain found that he could not dive because the boiler-room ventilators would not close: seas had smashed the second coxswain's paint locker in the funnel well, and a tin of paint had jammed under one of the mushroom-shaped ventilators. Conditions were far too rough for anyone to climb on deck to remove the tin. To make matters worse, the engine-room staff reported that the motor supplying fuel to the auxiliary diesel engine had broken down. Twice over a period of several hours the stokers relit the boilers; twice more the steep, short waves of a violent North Sea extinguished them. All this time the *Southampton* stood by the submarine, and in one abortive attempt to take her in tow she lost twelve men overboard. At one point the captain of K9 considered abandoning ship, but decided it was safer to stay with her. She rode out the gale, and the cruiser towed her into the Tyne for repairs before she continued to Chatham.

Back at Rosyth, Geoffrey Layton had just returned with K6 from Swan and Hunter's yard on the Tyne, where she had been the first of the boats to be fitted with the modified swan bows and to have her funnels lengthened to lessen the danger of high seas flooding the boilers. Commander William Crowther had joined the boat, and was to assume command from Layton after the next trip. K22, alias K13, also received a new officer and a visitor. Lieutenant Edmund Dodd joined her as first lieutenant, thus relinquishing a similar job on another submarine, K17. The visitor was Lieutenant-Commander Hubert Vaughan Jones, the captain of K15, which was nearing completion at Scott's yard at Greenock. He had been called to Rosyth and allocated to K22 to gain sea-going experience in the class. For the same purpose Lieutenant-Commander Athelstan Fenner, who was expecting any day to begin trials on K16 at Beardmore's Clydeside yard, was temporarily on board K4 at Rosyth. Only two weeks earlier both Vaughan Jones and Fenner had returned from the Baltic, where they had operated in E boats. On the night of Vaughan Jones's arrival at Rosyth he was invited to a small reunion party on K4. Several long-standing friendships were renewed and many yarns swapped. Layton joked with Stocks, telling him to keep his boat clear of K6's new bows in future if he valued his skin. Stocks laughingly replied that Layton had better watch where he was going, too, for since K4 had damaged her bows in the collision with K1 she had been fitted with a new steel stem-piece, four inches thick.

It was the evening of 30 January, exactly a year since the sinking of K13, and inevitably the men talked about the disaster and about Godfrey Herbert and Kenneth Michell, who had saved Herbert and the other survivors from the bottom of the Gareloch. Athelstan Fenner knew both men well. He had been with them on that record-breaking voyage to Hong Kong by three C-class submarines in 1911. Naturally enough, Vaughan Jones, Fenner and Crowther asked many questions about the K boats, and the other officers did their best to answer them objectively. But, as one of them said, to get to know a K boat there was nothing like first-hand experience; and they would be getting that tomorrow.

Operation E.C.1. was devised by Vice-Admiral Beatty with the partic-ular objects of exercising his cruiser squadrons and of practising deployments. It was also necessary to keep his bored fleet in fighting trim and there was always the hope that they might run into the enemy. E.C.1. was to be a full-scale affair. With Beatty in his flagship, *Queen Elizabeth*, the force from Scapa would consist of 26 battleships of the 1st, 2nd, 3rd, 4th, 5th, 6th and 8th divisions of the Battle Fleet, 9 cruisers, 4 light cruisers and numerous destroyers. The Rosyth base would provide the 3 battleships of the Fifth Battle Squadron, the cruisers *Courageous* and *Blanche*, the 2nd Battle Cruiser Squadron of 4 ships, the 14 ships of the 1st, 3rd and 4th Light Cruiser Squadrons, the two K-class submarine flotillas ,each led by a light cruiser, and again numerous destroyers. The two forces would meet somewhere in the North Sea and the exercise would take place through the night of 1 February.

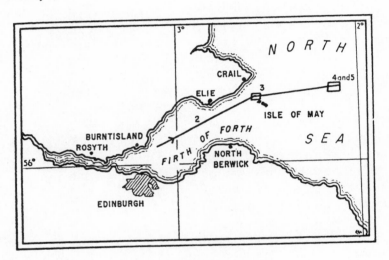

BATTLE OF MAY ISLAND (1)
The numbers 2–5 on the map indicate the locale for
the diagrams following (pp. 81–84)

Beatty sent out the orders for the exercise on 28 January, with instructions to the vice-admiral commanding the Rosyth force, Sir Hugh Evan-Thomas, to leave on the evening of 31 January. The planning of the order and times of the departure was left to Evan-Thomas and his senior officers. To navigate more than forty warships through the complicated defences of the Forth estuary in darkness, in radio silence and with each ship showing only one stern light was no mean performance. It called for a high level of skill, nerve and timing.

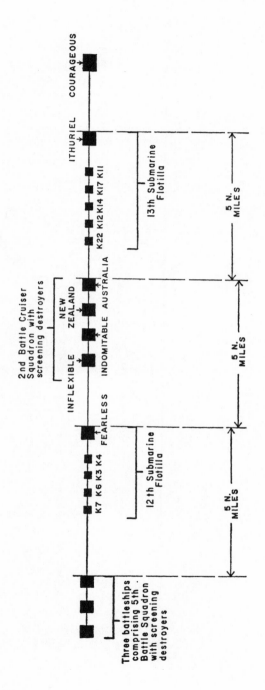

BATTLE OF MAY ISLAND (2)

Formation of leading units of the Rosyth force leaving the Firth of Forth.

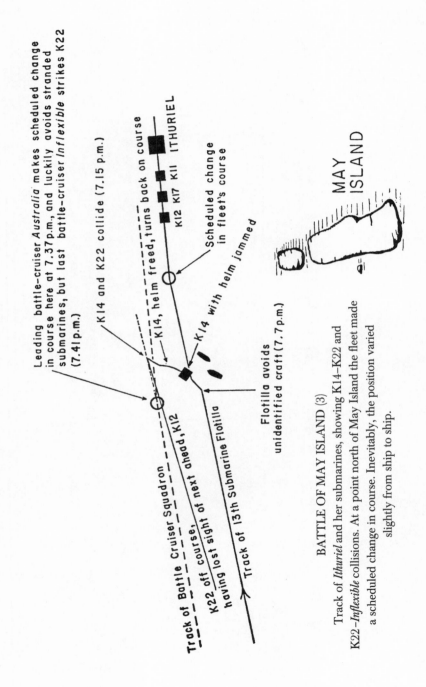

Leading battle-cruiser *Australia* makes scheduled change in course here at 7.37 p.m., and luckily avoids stranded submarines, but last battle-cruiser *Inflexible* strikes K22 (7.41 p.m.)

K14 and K22 collide (7.15 p.m.)

K14, helm freed, turns back on course

ITHURIEL

K12 K17 K11

Scheduled change in fleet's course

K14 with helm jammed

Flotilla avoids unidentified craft (7.7 p.m.)

Track of Battle Cruiser Squadron

K22 off course, sight of next ahead, K12 having lost sight of next ahead, K12

Track of 13th Submarine Flotilla

MAY ISLAND

BATTLE OF MAY ISLAND (3)

Track of *Ithuriel* and her submarines, showing K14–K22 and K22–*Inflexible* collisions. At a point north of May Island the fleet made a scheduled change in course. Inevitably, the position varied slightly from ship to ship.

82

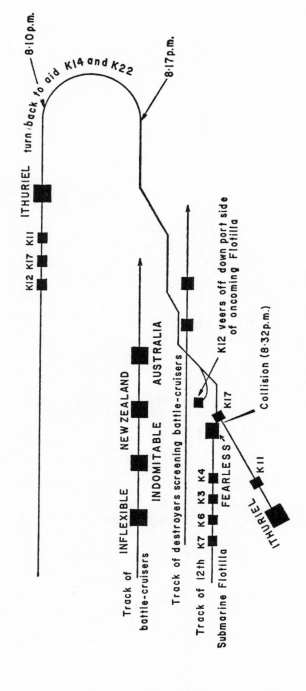

BATTLE OF MAY ISLAND (4)

The track of *Ithuriel* and her three remaining K boats, showing avoiding action and *Fearless*–K17 collision.

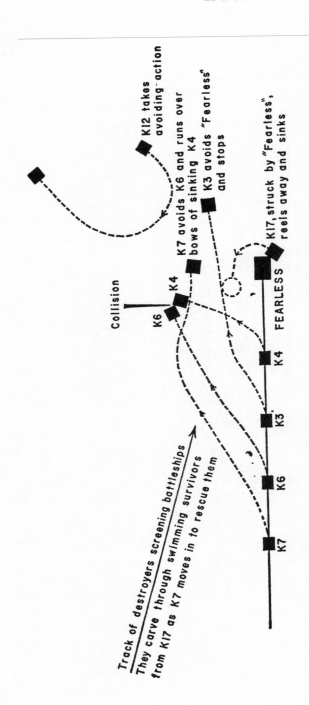

BATTLE OF MAY ISLAND (5)

Movements of the 12th Submarine Flotilla immediately after *Fearless* and K17 collided.

On the morning of 1 February the senior officers at Rosyth agreed on the final arrangements, then Evan-Thomas disembarked from the battleship *Barham* and hoisted his flat in *Courageous,* which was to lead the force. At half-past three in the afternoon he received a telephone message from *Barham* saying that fifty minutes earlier a Navy seaplane had spotted a U-boat five miles south-east of May Island, which lies at the mouth of the Forth estuary. The U-boat had dived before the seaplane could attack. Its reported position lay close to a channel through a minefield, a channel along which the fleet was soon to pass. Evan-Thomas decided to carry on with the operation, but to order the fleet to increase its speed to 22 knots for one hour after passing May Island. If the U-boat still lurked in the area this would ensure that it had only fast-moving targets. Later in the afternoon Evan-Thomas modified this instruction, reducing the speed after May Island by one knot.

Meanwhile Commander Leir, in *Ithuriel,* was ordered to lead his five K boats of the 13th Flotilla downriver and to anchor in Burntisland Roads. This was to assist the force in moving more smoothly out of the river.

At 6.30 p.m. the operation began. The night was clear, the sea calm, the temperature cold. The moon was not yet up. *Courageous* moved downstream, and Leir led his K boats in line astern behind her. Simultaneously, five miles up the river, the 2nd Battle Cruiser Squadron, consisting of *Australia, New Zealand, Indomitable* and *Inflexible,* got under way in that order and again in line astern. Down the estuary screening destroyers would join them. The next group to leave would be the 12th Submarine Flotilla, led by Captain Little in the cruiser *Fearless.* Little was timed to move with his four K boats when *Australia* was five miles distant. Spaced at similar intervals behind him would come the battleships, with more destroyers, and finally the light cruiser squadrons. With the entire force moving in line astern, the K boats would be positioned thus: *Courageous, Ithuriel,* K11, K17, K14, K12, K22, *Australia, New Zealand, Indomitable, Inflexible, Fearless,* K4, K3, K6, K7, followed by the battleships. The submarines were to travel about four hundred yards apart, each showing a blue stern light at half-brilliance. Blackout shields prevented these lights from being seen more than one compass point (11¼°) each side of the ship's centre-line.

On K22 the navigator, Lieutenant Laurence Dickinson, was officer of the watch. The captain, de Burgh, his new first lieutenant, Dodd, and the passenger, Vaughan Jones, were below in the wardroom. Vaughan Jones was lying on de Burgh's bunk. In the petty officers' mess Oscar Moth was attending to his paper work and intermittently chatting to a stoker petty officer named William Damerell.

'Wonder if there's something really brewing or if this is just another of Beatty's stunts?'

'Don't know. Couldn't find out a thing before we left. The captain will tell us when he's ready.'

Moth said, 'Anyway, I'm damn glad we didn't go out yesterday or the day before.'

'Why?'

'The 29th was the anniversary of the sinking in the Gareloch. A year ago yesterday I thought my number was up.'

The stoker petty officer grinned at Moth's bald pate. 'Instead of that you came up looking handsomer than ever, Mossy.'

Ahead of the K flotilla, *Courageous* passed through the Black Rock Gate, the opening in the inner boom defences. The boom spanned the estuary at a point six miles wide between Leith and Burntisland. *Courageous* signalled to *Ithuriel* to let her screening destroyers take station between the battle-cruiser and the flotilla leader. *Ithuriel* then followed 1,200 yards behind. The 13th Flotilla's speed was 16 knots. It was 6.33 p.m. At this precise moment, some twenty miles distant, a much smaller force of ships was moving into action, some of them directly in the path of the oncoming fleet. They were eight armed trawlers, sweeping for mines. Incredibly, neither their commander, Temporary Lieutenant Robinson Rigby, nor their reporting base on May Island had any information concerning Operation E.C.1. or the movements of the Grand Fleet.

At 6.41 the leading ships in the Rosyth force ran into a light, low-lying mist and the men on watch on *Ithuriel* lost sight of *Courageous*. Leir increased his speed to 17 knots, and nine minutes later to 19 knots. The submarines behind him following suit. *Courageous* did not show up.

By now *Ithuriel* was passing through the Fidra Gap, the gate in the estuary's outer defence boom. This boom stretched fifteen miles between Fidra Island, near North Berwick, and Elie Ness. Behind the K flotilla most of the force was now on the move, strung out in a line thirty miles long. While the leader was drawing clear of the estuary the last units had yet to pass under the Forth railway bridge. Everything was going smoothly.

The Isle of May, where the ships were to increase speed, lies just beyond a line drawn between the two outermost points of the estuary. It is five miles from the village of Crail, on the north shore, and ten miles from North Berwick, on the south shore. Slightly more than a mile long and a third of a mile across at its widest point, the island rises to 160 feet. It contains the remains of a twelfth-century priory, a light-house and, in time of war, naval and military installations.

At 7.06 *Courageous* passed the island a mile and a half away on her starboard beam, and raised her speed to 21 knots. At 7.10 *Ithuriel*, only a minute behind *Courageous* but still unable to see her stern light, made a slight change in course as scheduled in the fleet's orders. She was now heading almost due east. The mist had reduced visibility for ordinary navigation lights to about a mile and a half.

Three-quarters of a mile behind *Ithuriel*, Commander Thomas Cecil Benfield Harbottle, on the bridge of K14, was watching closely the stern lights of the two submarines ahead. Passing May Island, it seemed to him that the leading boat, K11, was reducing speed and hauling out to port. It was strange, he thought: now was the time that they should increase speed. The next moment K17, in whose wake Harbottle was accurately travelling, copied K11. Harbottle cut his speed from 19 knots to 13, but held his course. He peered intensely over the canvas bridge screen, wondering what could have made the two submarines swerve. Seconds later the silhouettes of two small craft showed half a mile ahead.

'What the devil are they?' Harbottle said to his signalman, William Fielder.

'They look like patrol boats, sir.'

The unknown boats, almost certainly two of the minesweeping trawlers, suddenly flashed on their navigation lights, and Harbottle realised that they were travelling in line ahead at a much slower rate than the submarine and along a course which would take them obliquely across her bows.

Harbottle ordered, 'Starboard fifteen.'

He realised immediately that he was gaining too fast on the two boats and would have to take more drastic evasive action. 'Hard a' starboard', he called.

In the wheelhouse under Harbottle's feet the helmsman, Able Seaman Harold Curtis, spun the wheel, and the bows of the submarine swung safely to port. But before Harbottle had time to make his next move the helmsman called out, 'The helm has jammed, sir.' Two degrees short of its full turning capacity, the steering-wheel had stiffened. Curtis could move it only three inches either way. The wheel felt as if it were held by two powerful opposing springs.

Harbottle switched on his navigation lights and commanded, 'Slow both engines.' He looked anxiously round to find the position of his next astern. At that moment, fortunately, K12 showed her navigation lights, and Harbottle saw thankfully that she would pass behind him.

Confident that de Burgh in K22 would be in the wake of K12, he concerned himself with getting well clear of the track of the battle-cruisers, now about four miles astern.

'Full speed port, slow starboard', he called, hoping to correct the swing to port and to draw away to the north shore of the estuary.

The next moment, however, Curtis reported that the helm had freed itself. It had been jammed for about six minutes. Harbottle decided to get back into the line. 'Hard a' port. Full speed ahead both.'

At the moment when the helm had jammed on K14 Lieutenant Dickinson, on watch on the other Fairfield-built boat, K22, lost sight of the stern light on his next ahead, K12. He kept the submarine on her course, north 65 degrees east.

Below, in the petty officers' mess, Oscar Moth was saying to Willie Damerell, 'It's a funny thing, Willie, twelve months this very night they got us out of this boat in the Gareloch. It was a bit later than this. About ten o'clock.'

Damerell said, 'If fate's going to have another go at us this year, then she'd better be quick.'

On the bridge Dickinson, his quartermaster, signalman and the lookout man strained for a sight of that elusive blue light on K12. Three minutes passed. Then, two hundred yards ahead on the starboard bow, a red navigation light sprang out of the night, moving across their path.

Dickinson reacted fast. 'Hard a' starboard!' he shouted.

But with K22 steaming at 19 knots and sluggish on the turn no reaction could have been fast enough. Even before she answered the helm she rammed the other boat.

The impact flung the three men on the bridge against the canvas screen and floored several of the crew inside the submarine. No one was hurt. The captain, de Burgh, dashed to the conning-tower ladder.

The orders from Dickinson rapped out. 'Stop engines. Close watertight doors.'

The men below swiftly obeyed. Someone switched on the navigation lights.

De Burgh clambered on to the bridge and demanded, 'What the hell have we hit?'

'I don't know, sir', Dickinson said. 'It might be K12. She came at us from the starboard, and I didn't see her till the last moment when she put her lights on.'

De Burgh, glancing back down the estuary, thought fast. 'Get a wandering lead with some lights on it round the back end of the conning-tower so that no one else runs into us, and get someone to go down and have a look at the bows. I'm going below to check on the doors. Try to find out who the hell we've hit.'

Down in the bows of K22 de Burgh found that a seaman had shut the foremost watertight door only fractionally in time. Through holes in the crumpled pressure hull water had flooded into the torpedo-room and surged like a torrent through the doorway into the next compartment. The door seemed to be holding well, but as an extra precaution de Burgh ordered several of the crew to shore up the whole bulkhead. By the time he got back to the bridge Dickinson was able to report that the other boat was a K boat, but he did not realise it was K14. He assumed it was K12.

The collision occurred on K14 at the moment after the steering freed itself, when Harbottle gave the order which would take him back into the line ahead formation. K22 sliced into her sister ship on the port side of the crew space, immediately behind the bow torpedo compartment. The blow severed part of the bows, including the forward wireless mast, and the water which burst into the crew space drowned instantly a leading seaman and an able seaman who sat off duty at a table. In the control-room the first lieutenant, a man named Gavin, anticipated his captain's order and leaped to the watertight door leading into the wardroom. Another door, made of wood and fitted to give the officers an extra touch of comfort, had splintered under the force of the collision and was jammed in the doorway. With water flooding towards him across the wardroom and over the door frame, Gavin saved himself, the rest of the crew and the submarine by wrenching the door from its hinges with a superhuman burst of strength and slamming home the watertight door. Then he reported to the bridge that the two forward compartments were flooded and that the watertight door in the control-room was holding.

Harbottle signalled by lamp to K22, asking de Burgh to report the collision and to seek help. De Burgh promptly sent a coded wireless message to *Ithuriel*: 'Priority. Have been in collision with submarine K12. Both ships are flooded forward.' It was then 7.15.

In answer to Harbottle, de Burgh signalled that K22 was all right and ready to proceed to harbour. But Harbottle replied telling him to stand by, because his boat was unable to move, well down by the bows and liable to sink at any moment.

De Burgh managed to manoeuvre his submarine slowly into a position with her head pointing along her original course. That way oncoming traffic ought clearly to see the array of lights behind the conning-tower. He stopped both engines.

On K14 the signalman on duty flashed out calls for help on the Aldis lamp, hoping that craft nearby might see them. Harbottle ordered another man to stand by with a Very pistol in his hand and a good supply of cartridges to warn off the ships coming up astern.

In the meantime *Ithuriel* and the other three submarines of the 13th Flotilla hurried away eastward, unaware of the accident. Like the submarines ahead of her, K12 had also to swerve to avoid the two unidentified craft, and when she resumed her station in the line she came up behind K17, thinking it was K14. More than an hour was to pass before *Ithuriel's* wireless department picked up, decoded and passed to Commander Leir the distress call from K22.

By 7.30, fifteen minutes after the collision, the four ships of the 2nd Battle Cruiser Squadron, with their escorting destroyers, were bearing down on the spot where K14 and K22 lay flashing and radioing calls for help into the night.

On the leading battle-cruiser, the 22,500-ton *Australia*, the order had just been given to increase speed to 21 knots when the men on the bridge sighted a red Very light arching into the sky well ahead on the port bow. It rose out of a bunch of lights at water-level. Almost immediately another light among them began flashing: 'H-a-v-e b-e-e-n i-n c-o-l-l-i-s-i-o-n. R-e-q-u-i-r-e a-s-s-i-s-t-a-n-c-e.' As *Australia* passed the bunch of lights well clear on her port beam Rear-Admiral Arthur Cavenagh Leveson, commanding the squadron, ordered the leader of the escorting destroyers, *Gabriel*, to detach one of his vessels to go to the assistance of the distressed ship. No one on the bridge of *Australia* realised that the signal had come from a submarine.

On K14 and K22 the men on the bridge and on the upper deck were going through a harrowing time as the battle-cruisers and their destroyers swept past them on both sides.

The last of the battle-cruisers was *Inflexible*. She had some time earlier lost sight of her next ahead, *Indomitable*. At half-past seven her navigator, Lieutenant-Commander Bernard Knightly Boase, saw Very lights rising out of the mist, and sent the officer of the watch, Lieutenant the Honourable John Bruce, to advise the captain. Captain James Rose Price Hawksley came on the bridge, but could make nothing of the Very shots through his binoculars. Then he saw two white lights and the starboard bow light of a small ship, and he told Bruce to take a bearing on them. Hawksley felt confident that *Inflexible* would pass clear of the lights. Next he saw a white light almost immediately ahead. Through his glasses he thought he could pick out the silhouette of *Indomitable*. The white light looked like her stern light, switched on at full power because of the misty conditions. The officer of the watch at first had the same impression. But then he and Boase suddenly called out, 'There's a green light. Hard a' port. Full speed astern starboard.'

Now Hawksley spotted the green light, too. Through his glasses it looked like some low-lying vessel. Boase thought it was a destroyer because it seemed to have a high forecastle. Whatever it was, the battle-cruiser, nearly two hundred yards long, was committed to hitting it. It lay less than four hundred yards away. And *Inflexible* was doing 18 knots.

In K22 Hubert Vaughan Jones, the visiting captain, stood at the foot of the conning-tower ladder. Oscar Moth had gone up on the bridge and with the others there had just stood transfixed as a destroyer swept by ten feet from the submarine's bows. A signalman began to flash a distress message to the destroyer when a shout came from aft. Everyone on the bridge turned his head. A hundred yards away the towering bows of a big ship were ploughing out of the darkness straight towards the engine-room. Below Vaughan Jones heard de Burgh thunder, 'Hard a' starboard. Full speed ahead starboard.' Exasperatedly, he yelled at the oncoming battle-cruiser, 'What the hell do you think you're doing?'

Inflexible began to turn away, but too late. She stormed into the already battered submarine, bending thirty feet of its bows like tinfoil, so that they stuck out to port at a right angle to the rest of the hull. The last-second orders of the men on *Inflexible* lessened the severity of the impact, but as her stern swung round she tore along the side of the submarine, wrenching away the external ballast and fuel tanks and pushing the whole boat down in the water till only the superstructure and bridge showed above the surface. The men clung desperately to the nearest handholds. A noise like an express train reverberated through the submarine, and those men still below, sensing what was happening, expected the bows of a ship and the sea to burst in on them. Oscar Moth thought he was about to die: call her K22, K13 or by any other name or number, he said to himself, she would never change. She was a killer.

The stern of the battle-cruiser bore down the side of K22 and the wash from the propellers swept over her; and then *Inflexible* drew clear and the submarine, though rocking wildly, was still afloat. The men on her saw the name on the stern of the big ship. A signaller flashed a message asking *Inflexible* to stand by. But the battle-cruiser rushed on unheeding into the night.

Inside K22 the various departments reported to de Burgh that they were still watertight. The bulkhead next to the damaged bows appeared to be holding well. The loss of the starboard ballast and fuel tanks caused the submarine to list to port, so de Burgh discharged 150 tons of ballast and fuel, mostly from tanks on the port side, to bring her on an even keel and to increase her buoyancy. He ordered more lights to be switched on fore and aft.

'If the blighters can't see us now, sir,' Moth said to him, 'they must be blind.' Close by, K14 lay miraculously afloat, too, letting off red Very shells at the rate of one a minute as surface ships raced perilously by.

The collision between K22 and *Inflexible* had occurred at 7.41. A minute earlier *Ithuriel*, now six miles away, at last picked up one of the intermittent coded distress calls from K22. Either the submarine's signalman or *Ithuriel's* coding officer partly used the wrong code, with the result that the message as handed to Commander Leir gave the impression that a steamer named *Nova Scotia* had collided with K12. While Leir pondered over the message a signal by Aldis lamp came from one of the submarines in the line, reporting that K22 had not been seen for some time. Was K12 or K22 in trouble? To the officers on the bridge of the flotilla leader the confusion was frustrating. Should they turn back to give assistance or not?

Twenty minutes after first receiving the coded distress call, *Ithuriel's* wireless office picked up a repeat of the message. This time the decoded version gave no reference to a steamer named *Nova Scotia*: it stated that K22 and K12 had collided. Leir decided to go back. It was the least he could do. In a collision a submarine has little chance of survival because of her low reserves of buoyancy. The two K boats carried more than a hundred men. To turn back to help them would have been out of the question if this had been a war operation; but it was an exercise. Lives were more important than manoeuvres.

Wherever *Ithuriel* went her charges had to go too; therefore a lamp signal went out to what was left of the flotilla to turn round or, more specifically, to make a sixteen-point turn to the southward in succession and using five degrees of helm. Leir switched on his navigation lights at full brilliance and a yardarm group of lights at the stern to assist the submarines on the turn. At ten minutes past eight he gave the order for the manoeuvre to begin. By making the turn with only five degrees of helm, he reckoned that he would pass safely to the south of the battle-cruisers and the rest of the force. At 8.17 the last submarine in the line, K12, completed the manoeuvre.

Meanwhile Leir sent for his coding officer and told him to transmit a radio message in code to *Courageous* and the battleship *Barham*, saying:

> Submarines K12 and K22 have been in collision and are holed forward. I
> am proceeding to their assistance with the 13th Submarine Flotilla. Position
> 18 miles eastward magnetic from May Island.

For some unexplained reason, the message did not leave *Ithuriel* for
a considerable time.

A minute after the flotilla completed its turn, at eighteen minutes
past eight, Leir was astonished to see the battle-cruiser *Australia*
coming towards him, almost dead ahead. The battle-cruiser squadron
was following a track farther south than that previously followed by
the K flotilla, and *Ithuriel* and the three submarines were now actually
cutting across the path of the battle-cruiser at a fine angle. Leir quickly
changed course to the south, and *Australia* passed *Ithuriel* six hundred
yards away on her starboard beam. But as the three submarines
manoeuvred with woeful sluggishness to follow their leader the
battle-cruiser was closing on them. In K12, the last in the line,
Lieutenant-Commander John Graham Bower suddenly saw *Australia*
bearing down on him out of the mist.

He gave a desperate order: 'Hard a' starboard.'

In *Australia* Rear-Admiral Leveson and his flag captain had spotted
Ithuriel and watched her turn away. But the last two submarines in the
line did not switch on their navigation lights until it was too late for
Australia to take evasive action. 'If we turn', Leveson said to his flag
captain, 'our stern will swing round and bang the last submarine on its
nose.' *Australia* held her course. With only two or three feet to spare,
K12 passed the battle-cruiser, and suffered only a rolling from her
bow wave.

Ahead *Ithuriel* was now dodging the destroyers escorting the battle-
cruisers. Having turned to avoid *Australia,* Leir sighted another set of
navigation lights right ahead. He swung *Ithuriel* sharply back to starboard and passed a destroyer close on his port side. Resuming his
south-westerly course, he found himself the next moment running into
another destroyer. Again a quick order pulled the flotilla leader away
in time, and she steamed across the destroyer's stern. In K11
Commander Thomas Frederick Parker Calvert and the men on the
bridge with him fully expected *Ithuriel* to hit both destroyers. How she
managed to miss them was little short of miraculous.

Within four minutes Leir had changed course five times. It would
have been futile and dangerous for the three submarines to try to
follow him. Each was temporarily on its own; and somehow each
weaved a safe path through the destroyers. After taking rapid avoiding
action K11 managed to resume her station four hundred yards behind

Ithuriel, which was now back on the course south 65 degrees west. K17, on the other hand, lost ground and fell about a mile behind K11.

In the three submarines word passed round that they had turned back to help two of their number after a collision. Reactions to the news varied. Some men were pleased at the prospect of going back to Rosyth; others were annoyed to be missing even make-believe action. At least one man had no views on the subject at all. He was Signalman George Kimbell, in K17. Kimbell had been ill in his bunk all day. At eight o'clock the navigating officer had gone aft to take his temperature and had told him to have a good sleep. That was a laugh. Every ten minutes Kimbell had to run to the water closet. He sat in there now feeling sorry for himself and telling himself that he wished he were dead.

Along the first leg of its journey, the Rosyth force had been able to maintain its line-ahead formation with a fair degree of accuracy, in spite of the darkness and the radio silence. All the ships were starting from approximately the same point, and were travelling along an estuary containing buoys and landmarks. But, as was to be expected, the groups of ships did not make the scheduled change in course beyond May Island all at precisely the same point. The result was that instead of steaming out across the North Sea in one long line they were moving in several short lines forming an irregular echelon. The battle-cruisers had changed course slightly before the position at which the first flotilla of K boats had turned; and they had therefore followed a track south of the K boats. That was why Leir had run among them when he turned round.

Five miles behind the battle-cruisers came the second group of K boats, the 12th Flotilla led by the light cruiser *Fearless.* Before she passed May Island, *Fearless* had intercepted the same coded distress call from K22 that *Ithuriel* picked up. That was just after a quarter to eight. *Fearless* was leading, K4, K3, K6 and K7, in that order. 'Tiny' Little, the tall, heavily-built captain of the flotilla, at once signalled the news of the collision to his submarines by Aldis lamp and warned them to keep a sharp look-out and to turn their stern lights to full brilliance.

At 7.54 *Fearless* passed May Island, and a few minutes later Little ordered the scheduled change in course at a position earlier than that at which the battle-cruisers had turned.

By 8.15 Little felt confident that he was well beyond the scene of the collision and that he could relax, relatively speaking.

At the same time in K6 Commander Geoffrey Layton finished his watch and went below to the wardroom for his dinner. Lieutenant Richard Douglas Sandford took over the bridge.

Still no signal had left *Ithuriel* warning the rest of the force that she and her submarines had turned round.

At 8.25 Rear-Admiral Leveson, in *Australia*, radioed to the three battleships behind the second group of K boats: 'Priority. Have just passed *Ithuriel* and three submarines inward bound.'

That signal, coming fifteen minutes after *Ithuriel* had begun to turn, was sent too late to warn *Fearless* and her submarines.

As the signal went out the officers on the bridge of *Fearless* sighted the white steering lights of two ships following one-another fine on the port bow, and passing in front of them from port to starboard. Almost immediately someone spotted the lights of a third vessel, about half a mile astern of the other two.

'Navigation lights', Little commanded. 'Signal the flotilla to show theirs too.' The message went out immediately by lamp and radio. Little and his men watched tensely as the lights of the first two ships crossed their bows, then they turned their attention to the third ship. Acting in accordance with the rule of the sea, Little held his course, confidently expecting the other vessel to port its helm and pass down his port side. *Fearless* and her K boats were steaming at 21 knots.

Half a dozen pairs of eyes on the bridge of the flotilla leader watched in awed fascination as the lights of the third ship moved inexorably ahead. What was the ship doing here anyway? Someone whispered, 'Turn, man, for God's sake, turn.' But the lights held their course.

'What's the damn fool playing at?' Little roared.

The next moment both vessels reached the positions where a collision became inevitable.

'Hard a' port. Full speed astern', Little shouted.

The ship's siren rent the night with three short blasts, then another three, indicating by the letter S in Morse code that she was going full astern. But she was not. The momentum from her high speed carried *Fearless* on, skidding towards the other vessel with horrifying sureness. The men in control were powerless now. The ship had taken over.

'It's K17, sir', someone yelled.

The next second *Fearless* slammed into her, burying her bows deep into the submarine forward of the conning-tower. The impact jarred the flotilla leader violently from stem to stern. Men were flung to the decks, and cracked their heads on machinery, bulkheads and furniture. Almost every compartment was thrown into a shambles.

The men on the bridge, prepared for the collision, steadied themselves, and watched K17 twist herself free and reel along the port side of the flotilla leader. She seemed to sink at once. For a few seconds the officers on the bridge of *Fearless* stood silent with shock. Then one had the wit to shout, 'Close all watertight doors.' Simultaneously Little ordered the letter D to be sounded on the siren, telling the boats coming up astern to keep clear. The time was 8.32.

K17 did not sink as quickly as the men on *Fearless* believed. In the darkness she drifted slowly astern of the flotilla leader. Water flooded through a great rent in her side at the foremost end of the wardroom.

In the stokers' mess in K17, five minutes before the collision, one of his mess-mates had pestered Stoker 1st Class Henry Fulcher to go with him up the conning-tower for a breather. Fulcher, just off watch and now reading a book, refused. He doubted anyway whether the officer of the watch would allow them on the bridge. But the other man insisted, and in the end Fulcher threw his book down and followed him. Another stoker, Albert Dowding, joined them. Aloft, there was never time for the officer on watch to reprove them or otherwise. The trio stepped on to the bridge as the collision occurred.

Ten seconds before the collision the bridge had ordered all watertight doors to be closed. The order saved at least one man's life, that of Lieutenant Gerald Armitage Jackson, who eight days earlier had replaced Lieutenant Dodd when he joined K22. Jackson was sitting on his bunk in the wardroom when he heard the order. He flung himself towards the door leading into the control-room as the bows of *Fearless* chopped through the pressure hull just behind him. The submarine rolled and kicked like a harpooned whale. Men fell in all directions. Jackson staggered through the door into the control-room and with a leading seaman named Anthony Westbrook tried to close it. But the rush of water was too powerful, sweeping them off their feet. The lights went out and clouds of gas rose from the flooded batteries.

From the beam tube torpedo-room, where he had been lying on his bunk, Stoker Petty Officer James Stewart scrambled through the door into the control-room and helped an able seaman named Drake to close it.

The man who had been sick all day, Signalman Kimbell, was returning along the boiler-room passage to the beam torpedo-room after yet another visit to the water closet. The order to close the doors stopped him in his tracks, and the collision sent him sprawling. With considerable presence of mind, he hurried back to the engine-room.

In the crew's quarters at the after end of the submarine, Leading Seaman Frederick Brown was climbing into his bunk when the crash came. He went to his locker, collected his lifebelt and, with the other men in the compartment, hurried through to the engine-room.

All over the boat men went quickly but coolly about their business. No one was hurt. No one panicked.

Above: *Swordfish*, the first British submarine with a funnel. Two years in building, not the least of her faults was a tendency to roll over.

Below: K8 making spray at speed in calm water. The inadequate canvas screens on the conning-tower eventually were replaced with streamlined steel screens. (*Imperial War Museum*)

Bottom: K3, the first K boat to be launched, driving through a choppy Irish Sea on her trials. Later in the day she was fired on – by a British armed trawler.

Above: K3 entering a floating dock after diving out of control and hitting the sea-bed. Prince George, later George VI, was on board at the time. *(Imperial War Museum)*

Above: K4 began her tragic existence by running aground on Walney Island, off Barrow-in-Furness, during her trials. *(Photo "Mirrorpic")*

K8 hove to while crew members retrieve a practice torpedo. K8 held the record among the class for the fastest dive – 3 minutes 25 seconds. *(Imperial War Museum)*

K7 in dry dock. One of the less pleasant discoveries in the K boats was to find the hydroplanes jammed during a dive.

Above: K13 on her acceptance trials, 29 January 1917. Three hours later she was trapped on the bottom of the Gareloch with more than thirty of her crew dead.

Below: K2. Built at Portsmouth Dockyard, her career began with an explosion and fire during her trials. (*Imperial War Museum*)

Below: K7 wearing her new swan bows, which were fitted to all the class when it was found that the original bows had insufficient buoyancy. (*Imperial War Museum*)

Above: K3 coming alongside a submarine parent ship. The Navy classed the giant K boats as self-contained, so the men had to live aboard even in port. *(Imperial War Museum)*

Above: George V leaves K1 after an inspection at Scapa Flow. The funnels were retracted to 'fool the Hun.'

Below: K6 on trials in Plymouth Sound. Devonport Dockyard men refused to dive in her after an underwater mishap in the tidal basin. *(Imperial War Museum)*

The light cruiser *Fearless* at Rosyth after ramming and sinking K17 at the Battle of May Island. Moments before *Fearless* struck K17 she was doing 21 knots.

In the cruiser no one was hurt. From the submarine only eight survived.

Above: Her trials over, K6 returns to Devonport. Later, at the Battle of May Island, she collided with and sank K4. *(Imperial War Museum)*

Above: K26. The last of the class. Much modified, much vaunted, she developed so many faults on a cruise to the Far East that the Admiralty decided never to put a funnel on a submarine again.

Below: K12 at speed near Portland, now fitted not only with swan bows but with a special forward gun mounting. In a seaway it was impossible to man the gun in its original position on the foredeck. *(Photo "Mirrorpic")*

Bottom: K12 in the Tyne returning from her trials. Once she clocked 24.2 knots on the surface for 72 miles.

Above: K14 calls at Southend on the *Victory Cruise* in 1919. It was the jamming of her steering which precipitated the accidents known as the Battle of May Island.

Above: K16 at speed off Portland. Her funnels were longer than those of other boats in the class. (*Photos "Mirrorpic"*)

Below: K5. Built at Portsmouth Dockyard, she dived during exercises with the Atlantic Fleet in January 1921 – and was never seen again. (*Imperial War Museum*)

K22 – the former K13 salved and refitted – lowering her funnels and trimming down for diving. Once she dived with her funnels up. Her collision with K14 was the first of the accidents in the Battle of May Island.

While Jackson and Westbrook, waist-deep in surging water, struggled vainly with the watertight door, an order came from the bridge to abandon ship. From the control-room and the engine-room the men clambered up the ladders and through the hatches on the upper deck of the submarine.

They gathered on the bridge and the superstructure.

The first lieutenant reported to the captain, 'Everywhere forward of the control-room is flooded, sir. The door into the beam torpedo-room is closed.'

The Chief E.R.A. reported that every man was on deck.

By now the bows of the submarine were awash.

The captain ordered everyone aft.

The stern slowly tilted out of the water as Jackson, in stockinged feet, and about twenty other men clambered along the superstructure. Some men perched themselves on top of the gun and the funnels.

The captain shouted, 'Where's Cooper? Fetch a lamp, Cooper.' Cooper was the signalman. The captain called for him four times. There was no answer.

The forward half of the submarine slid under water, and the sea began to wash men overboard like flies off a lettuce leaf. The scene was uncanny: under a starry sky, K17 was disappearing beneath a calm sea, and most of her crew were accepting their fate in stunned silence. Only a few cried for help. A small searchlight on *Fearless* stabbed into the darkness, then swung round till its beam cut across the sinking submarine. Some men waved.

Stoker 1st Class Kenneth Vass watched the captain take off his jacket and prepare to jump into the water. Vass himself then dived overboard.

Lieutenant Jackson was washed off before he reached the stern. He swam away from the boat, then turned on his back momentarily and saw her silhouetted stern pointing to the sky.

Other men still clung to the submarine. One of them was Leading Seaman Westbrook. He and the quartermaster had climbed on to the uptilted stern. Around them they could see the lights of several ships. Suddenly Westbrook remembered that he was wearing his sea-boots.

'Help me pull off my––'. But the quartermaster had gone. So Westbrook sat on the stern and, as water gurgled up to meet him, pulled off his boots.

Eight minutes after *Fearless* had struck her, K17 slid out of sight to the sea-bed, twenty-seven fathoms down.

Four hundred yards behind *Fearless*, Commander Stocks in K4 heard the flotilla leader's siren signalling 'full astern' and stopped his engines. He switched on his navigation lights, put his stern light to full brilliance, and, as the submarine closed with *Fearless*, turned her to starboard, unaware that there had been a collision.

On the next astern, K3, Sub-Lieutenant Laurence Fitzgerald Foley was on watch. When the lights appeared on the ships ahead he turned on K3's navigation lights and sent a message below to the captain, who was at dinner. Lieutenant-Commander Herbert William Shove, the man who kept a tame white rat in his monkey jacket, promptly went up to the bridge. By now more than one siren seemed to be sounding, and it was impossible to distinguish the signals. But K3 was clearly gaining on K4 and Shove halved his speed. He wondered why Stocks was disregarding orders and showing his stern light at full brilliance.

Suddenly both Shove and Foley exclaimed as they realised that they were coming up on K4 so rapidly that in a matter of seconds they would hit her. Shove went hard to port and narrowly missed K4. He righted his helm to prevent the sterns of the two submarines coming together, then ordered full astern. A quarter of a mile on, K3 came to a stop. All the time Shove peered anxiously ahead, wondering what was causing the commotion. He could see nothing.

A shout from behind made him turn. On his starboard beam *Fearless* was throwing a searchlight aft. He and Foley were astounded to see, silhouetted in the rays of the searchlight, a submarine sinking with a crowd of men standing on her stern, waving their arms.

Shove decided not to try to rescue the men. Two other K boats were much nearer to them. He would only add to the confusion.

Ithuriel and K11 proceeded on their errand of mercy to the scene of the first collision utterly unaware of the mounting havoc behind them. The officers of the watch in both vessels had sighted the lights of *Fearless*, and indeed K11 had manoeuvred to give her a wide berth; but there had never been cause for alarm.

Only that one submarine still trailed obediently in the wake of the flotilla leader. K22 and K14 had collided miles back. *Fearless* had sunk K17. And even now the last in the depleted line of the 13th Flotilla, K12, having narrowly missed *Australia*, was ploughing along a collision course towards K6, the third in the line of the 12th Flotilla.

Fortunately, the men on watch in the two boats, Lieutenant-Commander Bower in K12, and Lieutenant Sandford in K6, each saw the lights of the other in time, and took evasive action. Both turned to starboard.

Then Sandford resumed his proper course. Hitherto he had been following about six hundred yards behind his next ahead, K3. In avoiding K12, he had briefly taken his eyes off K3, but now he saw a white light ahead and resumed station behind it, still travelling at 18 knots. Somewhere ahead he could hear a ship's siren sounding the letter 'D'. He sent below for the captain.

The next moment the lieutenant was perplexed to see a ship's starboard light off his port bow. He realised at once that the white light he had been following was not K3's stern light. It was the steaming light of this other vessel, which was apparently crossing his bows.

At that moment the captain, Commander Geoffrey Layton, came on the bridge. The submarine was now closing rapidly with the vessel in front.

'Slow both', Layton shouted. 'Stop both.'

Ahead, darkly silhouetted, lay a submarine stopped broadside on to the path of K6.

'Full speed astern. Hard a' port. Sound full astern on the siren. Navigation lights on, searchlight on astern.'

All Layton could hope to do was to make the collision a glancing blow.

In *Fearless* Staff Surgeon Aloysius Francis Fleming had been sitting in the wardroom when the flotilla leader hit K17. He hurried to his cabin, picked up his hat and lifebelt and went on the quarterdeck. Astern, on the starboard quarter, he saw a K boat caught in the beam of a searchlight shining from *Fearless*. The submarine was showing her navigation and steaming lights, and Fleming wondered why she had stopped and was lying broadside on to the path of the flotilla. He had been watching her for about a minute when a geyser of water plumed into the air near her after funnel. It looked like an explosion. Nothing happened for a moment or two, then the submarine began to sink. She went down in less than a minute. Fleming stood with his eyes rooted unbelievingly on the black patch of water where the K boat had been. It had happened so fast that a man could well wonder if he had imagined it.

'Good Lord', he muttered. 'A Hun torpedo.'

At once he assumed that a torpedo had caused the thunderous crash on *Fearless* a moment or two ago. Perhaps even now she was sinking. He hurried forward to the sick bay to get the men there into their lifebelts and ready to abandon ship.

But, of course, no German torpedo had struck the submarine in the searchlight. She was K4; and she had been rammed by her sister ship, K6, only a few yards from the spot where K17 had gone down.

Though the engines of K6 were going full speed astern, she had so much way on that the twin propellers hardly checked her. Her new swan bows met K4 at a right angle and almost cut her in half. The two submarines locked themselves so tightly together that K6's engines could not pull her free. The boats lay momentarily poised on the water, then K4 began to sink rapidly, carrying K6 down with her. Layton closed all watertight doors and flashed a message to *Fearless* saying he had collided with another submarine and needed help urgently.

For thirty agonising, timeless seconds his mind raced with possible moves he could make. Then the threshing propellers of K6 and her greater buoyancy broke her out of K4. She bounced back to her normal trim, and Layton stopped his engines, detailed Sandford to examine the fore compartments, and turned on his searchlight aft as a warning to the last in the line, K7.

By then only the bridge of K4 remained above the water.

Lieutenant-Commander Gravener, the former E-boat man who had not found his K boat command as pleasing as expected, stood on watch on the bridge of K7 when he first heard the letter D repeatedly sounding on a siren far ahead. K7 was lying half a mile behind K6. In his short period with the flotilla Gravener had become aware of the phenomenon known as losing suction which brought a K boat unexpectedly to a halt. With this in mind he always put an extra hundred yards on the stipulated distance between his submarine and the next ahead. The habit brought him regular rebukes from the flotilla commander. But Gravener, who made the excuse that he was a poor judge of distance, consoled himself with the knowledge that it was a habit which helped to keep himself and his crew alive.

Half a minute after first hearing the siren Gravener reduced his speed to 12 knots and switched on his navigation lights. Ahead and to starboard he recognised the lights of a cruiser which turned out to be *Fearless*. Ahead and to port was K6, which, Gravener presumed, was still moving forward. To give the cruiser plenty of room, he turned to port. Straight away he found himself closing with K6.

'Stop engines', he ordered. But the faint silhouette and the lights of the other submarine came rapidly nearer. Good Lord, Gravener thought, we're going to ram her. She must have stopped.

'Hard a'starboard', he called to the helmsman. 'Full astern both engines.'

Just in time, the full helm pulled the nose of the submarine clear. K7 swept close down the starboard side of K6, and Gravener gave a sigh of relief. But the feeling was short-lived. As K6 switched on her searchlight Gravener was appalled to see another submarine across her bows. He could do nothing to avoid it. He saw the whole boat clearly: bows, bridge, funnel, superstructure and stern. There was no sign of life. But something was wrong. The silhouette was slipping downwards.

'Hell, it's sinking', Gravener cried.

It was fantastic. The submarine went down so fast that the forward end of K7's keel only lightly touched its bows.

Gravener stopped his engines and looked around, utterly confused. On his port beam, astern of the submarine which had just sunk, he could hear men shouting and splashing in the water. *Fearless* shone a searchlight on some of them and signalled to Gravener to try to pick them up. Calling on deck as many spare hands as were available, he went slowly astern.

Four miles behind the last K boat came the three battleships of the Rosyth force, the 5th Battle Squadron.

At 7.54 the leading battleship, *Barham,* had picked up a radio signal from the battle-cruiser *Australia,* saying: 'Vessel in distress in path of fleet due north of May Island. Destroyer standing by.' The message, which referred to K14 and K22, was the first general radio warning about the accident. It went out **forty** minutes after the collision had occurred, **twenty** minutes after *Australia* had passed the scene of the accident and **thirteen** minutes after *Inflexible* had clouted K22. Still no sound had come from the wireless room of the flotilla leader, *Ithuriel.*

At 8.09 the three battleships passed May Island. By then the destroyer *Venetia* had closed with K14, lowered a boat to stand by her and thrown a searchlight on her. As a result the 5th Battle Squadron and all the ships behind passed the two crippled submarines in safety.

Beyond May Island the battleships and their screening destroyers duly changed course. Fifteen minutes later, just after half-past eight, came the three collisions which sank K17 and K4, and left one crippled cruiser and four K-class submarines in the path of the battleships in an agony of confusion, bewilderment and indecision.

As the heavy ships drew near, K3 stood on the port beam of *Fearless* with K6 and K7 behind them. K12, from the other flotilla, was thoroughly baffled by the events, and had turned round and stopped on K3's port bow. In the calm, icy water, amid these five ships which by now showed a galaxy of lights and made a handsome target for a U-boat, many of the 56 members of the crew of K17 were still swimming around, hoping to be rescued.

At 8.38, immediately after her collision, *Fearless* sent a priority radio signal to *Barham,* reporting that she had sunk K17.

Two minutes later *Ithuriel* at long last began to transmit the message saying that she and her submarines had turned back to help K22 and K14. By now, of course, only K11 trailed behind her.

Neither message gave the battleships time to alter course. At 21 knots the three of them thundered through the stationary remnants of the K flotillas. One after the other they missed the bows of K3 by the thickness of a piece of armour plate. But no collisions occurred.

Simultaneously the escorting destroyers ploughed towards *Fearless* and K7. At the time Gravener was moving K7 gently astern with his men spread along the upper deck ready to help the survivors from K17. Some of his crew were stripping off their clothes to dive overboard to help their comrades. The first of the survivors had just been lifted on to the submarine when the escorting destroyers swept over the spot where K17 had gone down. In three terrible minutes they ran down, cut to pieces and washed away the majority of the men from K17. Their wash knocked overboard several men from K7, but all managed to clamber back.

Over the next half-hour Gravener managed to find nine men from K17. From *Fearless*, Little sent Staff Surgeon Fleming by whaler to give the men medical attention. One of them was dying. The doctor strove for two hours in the wardroom of the submarine to revive him, but it was in vain. Of the remaining eight survivors, three required medical attention. All were put to bed in the submarine with liberal doses of rum and layers of blankets. Their names were Lieutenant Jackson, Stoker Petty Officer Stewart, Stokers 1st Class Fulcher, Dowding and Vass, Leading Seaman Brown and Westbrook, and the sick signalman, George Kimbell.

It was remarkable, though understandable, that for some time confusion reigned over the identity of the second sunken submarine. Layton in K6 first signalled to *Fearless* that he had run down K3, an assumption made because she was his next ahead. But then K3 identified herself on the port beam of the flotilla leader. When Layton heard that *Fearless* herself had been in a collision he decided that K6 had struck K17 as she was sinking.

But to the officers on the bridge of *Fearless* it was soon apparent that K4 had disappeared.

In K6 Lieutenant Sandford reported to his captain that the fore compartment was flooded to a depth of six inches, but that the leak, which was in the starboard lower torpedo tube, had been stopped and the water was being pumped out. Layton signalled by lamp to *Fearless* that he was in no danger after all.

About half an hour after the collision Captain Little ordered K3 and

K12 to return to harbour. In the meantime, boats had put out from *Fearless* to search for more survivors. They were away for an hour. The moon had not yet risen above the clouds on the horizon, and, though there was a clear, bright, starlit sky above, the smooth surface of the sea was black and unrevealing. The searchers found no one.

The collision with K17 had hacked a giant slice from the bows of *Fearless* and flooded a number of her lower compartments. Some twenty feet of the top half of the bows overhung the water. On the starboard side a huge, jagged piece of plating stuck out like a fin. When Little tried to move the ship ahead this plating turned her against the helm. Two hours after the accident, at 9.49, he flashed to Gravener in K7: 'I am going to return up harbour, stern first, at slow speed. Keep near me.'

For half an hour both K7 and K6 kept station with *Fearless* as she steamed at 3½ knots back up the estuary. When it became clear that the exposed watertight doors at the bows would hold and that she was in no danger, Little sent the two submarines on ahead to anchor in Burntisland Roads.

All this time *Ithuriel* and K11 had proceeded unwittingly on their tragic and needless errand of mercy to K22 and K14. When they arrived north of May Island at 9.15, K22 had already left stern first for Rosyth, escorted by an armed trawler; and K14, with what was left of her bows well under water, was about to follow, towed by the destroyer *Venetia*. *Ithuriel* accompanied them as far as Inchkeith, where a harbour tug took over the towing.

Neither the two crippled submarines nor *Fearless* reached Rosyth until well after dawn on 1 February. Daylight revealed a piece of plating from K17 embedded in the flotilla leader's bows, and on closer examination it showed that *Fearless* had struck her near her foremost bulkhead.

That day, in the outer estuary of the Forth, a search went on specifically for wreckage from K4. The sea gave up several bodies of men from K17 but not a trace of anyone or anything from the other submarines.

On the night of 1 February, far out in the North Sea, the Grand Fleet carried out the exercise Operation E.C.1. on schedule. The absence of the K boats made little difference. Beatty got back to Scapa Flow the next day and ordered an inquiry into the disaster. Three days later at Rosyth, aboard the battleship *Orion*, the proceedings began before Rear-Admiral William Edmund Goodenough and Captain Walter Maurice Ellerton. During the five days that the inquiry lasted a ditty box and a drawer from the crew's quarters in K4 were picked up east of May Island. On 9 February the court finished its investigation and submitted its findings to Beatty, blaming five officers from the K flotillas for the collisions. One was later court-martialled and severely reprimanded.

The decisions of the court did not satisfy many crew members of the K flotillas. Unlike the court of inquiry, they could not ignore the unsolved mysteries, the welter of coincidence and the background of ill-luck. The acting engineer lieutenant of K14, Thomas Gardener, had told the court that on the return journey to harbour he could find nothing wrong with the submarine's steering-gear. He tried to jam it deliberately without success. In dry-dock at Rosyth four naval and civilian engineers inspected the steering. They found neither defect nor foreign bodies; and all the helm readings were accurate. Gardener advanced a theory, supported by the other engineers, that the gear might have stuck if the wheel had been spun at tremendous speed. But it would have jammed only for half a second.

So what force had prevented the helmsman, Harold Curtis, 'a very able man,' from turning the wheel for six minutes? K14 was a Fairfield-built boat. So was K22, alias K13, which collided with her. The accident occurred on the anniversary of the loss of K13. And in a sense it was the hapless K22 which triggered off the entire tragedy because if she had not run off course she would never have struck K14. In the wide expanse of the estuary, was it not strange that K22 should lose sight of.her next ahead, that simultaneously the steering on her sister ship should jam and that from positions a half a mile apart they should converge on one-another? As Oscar Moth had said, who dare say now that K13 was not a killer? You did not change a ship by changing her name.

There was even further food for superstitious thought in the evidence at the inquiry of the captains of three minesweeping trawlers. These were the vessels which were believed to have got in the way of the first line of submarines, causing them to swerve and K14's steering to jam. All three captains vowed that during their sweep that night they had seen and heard nothing of the K flotillas or, for that matter, of the entire Rosyth force. Did the submarine officers see the lights of the trawlers? If not, what lights caused them to swerve?

All the unanswered questions weighed heavily in the arguments of some superstitious submariners.

The submission of the court of inquiry on the collision between *Inflexible* and K22 blamed the captain of K22, Lieutenant-Commander de Burgh, because his crippled submarine lay in the track of the outgoing units of the Rosyth force. The court knew that K22 was holed and standing by K14, but someone had to be blamed; and it is not without significance that, even though K22 was well-lit and flashing continuous distress signals, the court chose not to attach any blame to the captain of the battle-cruiser. Beatty, however, did not accept the finding and recommended 'No action'.

Immediately after the accident the captain of *Fearless,* Charles Little, wrote in his report: 'I know it will be felt that the flotilla made a mess of a difficult situation . . .' And this was precisely the view of the naval hierarchy. The First Lord of the Admiralty, Sir Eric Campbell Geddes, wrote as follows to the First Sea Lord:

> I cannot but think as a layman that this chapter of accidents looks as if there was something wrong with the standard of efficiency of the officers. Of course, naval officers will better appreciate the difficulties than I, but broadly speaking the catastrophe was caused by the cumulative mistakes of the majority of those concerned.

No-one at the Admiralty and no flag officer ever entertained the thought of blaming the machines or the system under which they operated. The concept of fleet submarines was inviolate. So were the K boats. The fault had to lie with those in charge of them.

But for the younger, more elastic minds of the K boat officers themselves the causes of the Battle of May Island, as the disaster came to be called, were clear and simple: the K boats had not the manoeuvrability, the range of visibility or the navigational aids necessary in vessels operating with the fleet. It was widely said of them that they had 'the speed of a destroyer, but the turning circle of a battle-cruiser and the bridge-control facilities of a picket-boat'. The Battle of May Island showed that submarines could not safely work with surface craft. Indeed, they could not work in flotilla formations by themselves without a drastic revision of the navigational systems. But these lessons were learned only by the submariners.

After the court of inquiry and the court-martial, several officers from the K flotillas went to new appointments. Harbottle took over an L-class submarine. Lieutenant Jackson, the only officer to survive from K17, left the flotilla after serving actively with it for precisely eight days. De Burgh was appointed to command the new K16 in succession to Fenner, who had died in K4. De Burgh asked his coxswain, Oscar Moth, to join him, but Mossy declined to chance his luck a third time in K boats. He went instead to the L class. Layton travelled south, as planned, to become assistant to Sydney Hall, the Commodore (Submarines). Before he left, of course, he handed over K6 to Lieutenant-Commander Crowther, who had sailed for the first time in a K boat on the night of the Battle of May Island. It was, as Layton told him afterwards, 'a bloody good introduction to K boats'.

CHAPTER SIX

THE RELUCTANT DIP-CHICK

What can submarines do? They can be built to do anything that a surface ship can do and can 'get there' unseen in order to do it, but when there they cannot do it so well. – Submarine Administration, Training and Construction, published by the Technical History Section of the Admiralty, 1921.

The short voyage from Rosyth to May Island and back had been an anticlimax for the passenger in K22, Lieutenant-Commander Hubert Vaughan Jones. Having been assigned to her to gain sea-going experience in the class, he was little the wiser when he returned to his own boat K15, which was nearing completion on the Clyde. The death of his friends, Fenner and Stocks, grieved him, but about the boats themselves he was not at all disheartened.

An experienced submarine captain, Vaughan Jones was impressed by the K class. For K15 he had a poetic motto in Latin specially engraved on a brass plate. Literally translated it read: 'Though I descend to the depths I arise more beautiful.' It was a thrilling occasion for him in April 1918 when he gave the order 'slow astern both' to take K15 from Scott's fitting-out berth at Greenock into the estuary on her trials. Admittedly he had an anxious moment or two wondering whether he could work her stern up against the strong ebb tide before her bows cleared the dock, but she behaved magnificently and was soon steaming towards the measured mile of Skelmorlie. There, without fuss or vibration, she exceeded her contract speed.

At about the same time Charles de Burgh, who had accommodated Vaughan Jones in K22, began trials in K16, which Beardmore's had built on Clydeside. Unfortunately, she behaved much less docilely than K15. Off Skelmorlie as she turned at speed for the second leg along the measured mile, her steering-gear failed, and at 25 knots she drove straight towards the beach. By reversing both engines the navigator checked her, though not a moment too soon. The fault was traced to the hydraulic system and repaired. More excitement came when the submarine arrived in the Gareloch for her diving trials. De Burgh chose to trim her down off the Shandon Hydropathic Hotel at the spot where K13 had gone down, and where he had dived her again as K22. Now, with the electric motors running slow ahead, he set K16's forward hydroplanes hard to dive and the after hydroplanes hard to rise. Without warning she put her nose down and plummeted towards the bottom of the loch. Orders came fast. 'Blow A.' 'Blow B.' 'Blow C.' 'Blow all tanks.' But nothing would stop her. With the depth gauge registering 112 feet, she furrowed into the sea-bed. Her stern kicked high out of the surface of the loch, then disappeared as she settled on an even keel. When the tanks emptied she surfaced with nothing more than superficial damage to the caps on her bow torpedo tubes. The mishap occurred because the after hydroplanes were not answering to the wheel.

With the kinks duly ironed out, the Navy took delivery of both submarines, and they sailed to Rosyth. It was now May 1918. Seventeen K boats had been commissioned since August 1916. K1, K4 and K17 had been lost, two were undergoing repairs and several of the remainder were due for modification. Both K flotillas were now used exclusively in the North Sea on what was called the K.K. patrol, the object of which was to give warning by radio of the movements of enemy vessels so that surface ships could lie in wait for them and press home an attack. No longer were the K boats themselves allowed to fire shots in anger. Each submarine patrolled for a week at a time, diving by day, surfacing and radioing at night. With never a promise of action, it was a boring job. The only excitements were produced by the boats themselves.

On the first night that Vaughan Jones took the new K15 out to the K.K. patrol line a north-easterly gale blew up. The boat was steaming along a course nearly beam on to the wind and in the short, steep seas she was rolling and labouring when several waves washed clean over the after part of the funnel superstructure. Water filled the casing, and the air intake fans sucked a solid stream into the boiler-room. In seconds it put out the furnace fires. Vaughan Jones shut off the submarine for diving, but not before the water had flooded the boiler-room, overflowed into the engine-room and created a negative buoyancy in the after end. Slowly she began to sink by the stern. All this happened in under four minutes. Nothing Vaughan Jones could do would stop the submarine from going down. He glanced at the chart to check the depth of the water, stopped the engines and waited. Eighty feet down her tail came gently to rest on the sea-bed.

Through the raised periscope Vaughan Jones could see the swan bows floating on the surface like a giant balloon. There should have been no difficulty in ejecting the water with the electric bilge pumps, but when they were switched on the level did not drop. A stoker volunteered to dive into the seven feet of oily water, and reported that cotton waste was embedded in the strainers on the suction pipes in the bilges. Several men stripped and went down in relays with knives to clear the obstruction. Eventually they got the pumps to work, but not for long. So much cotton waste was floating in the water that the strainers had to be cleared several times before all of it was removed. Eight hours after it had gone down K15's stern floated to the surface.

Seven days later Vaughan Jones returned from the patrol to learn the galling fact that a defect which had helped to cause the trouble was well known, and had been remedied on all boats but his. Much of the water had entered the funnel superstructure through the freeing ports which, idiotically, opened both ways. The modification ensured that the ports allowed water to pass only out of the superstructure.

Though this was the first recorded time that a K boat had dived stern first out of control, the flotillas had lost count of all the accidental and erratic submergences. It was fortunate, of course, that the boats operated only in the North Sea, where for the most part the water was not deep enough for a sinking submarine to come to harm from excessive pressure. Only one spot in their routine operational area was dangerously deep: situated in the Pentland Firth, it was known to submariners as the 'pot-hole'. Sure enough, the day came when a K boat dived into it.

It happened on 2 May, 1918. The boat, captained by Shove, the man with the pet white rat, got out of hand while trimming for diving. She hit the sea-bed at a depth of 266 feet. The high pressure damaged her along her entire length. Stays, angles and stanchions were buckled, plating was crumpled and the rudder and hydroplane gears were distorted; but she surfaced safely and put into Newcastle-upon-Tyne for repairs. 'The cause of the accident', the official report said, ' is not clear.'

On 10 June, 1918, the Admiralty demonstrated its continuing and unshakeable faith in the K class by ordering six more boats, three each from the yards of Armstrong Whitworth and Vickers. They were to be numbered K23 to K28.

Undeterred by the tragi-comic record of the K class, the top naval minds were determined that the large submarine had come to stay. Indeed, they believed that when engine design improved submarines would grow still larger than the K boat. The theory seemed to be that the bigger the submarine the more potent it would be. Lord Fisher had much to do with this frame of mind. The success of the German

U-boats had proved that he had not underestimated the destructive power of the submarine. He had been right and most of the other Sea Lords wrong. Now, though he had retired, no one cared to ignore him; and while he remained critical of the use of steam-engines he pursued with all his ardour the idea of the submarine battleship. By mid-1918 much time, money and half-baked thinking had gone into its development.

It was on 5 August of 1915, only three months after his resignation, that Fisher had originally put to the First Lord, Arthur Balfour, a plan for 'a submarine dreadnought' with a 12-inch gun mounted in front of its conning-tower in addition to the normal torpedo armament. Fisher believed that the gun would be far more accurate, reliable and damaging than the torpedo, which was hopelessly ineffective. British torpedoes did everything except sink enemy ships. They ran on the surface and were easily avoided; they ran too deep and passed under the targets; they broke down on the way and sank; and they failed to explode on contact.

In April 1915 Fisher had written to Jellicoe, saying: 'The *Vernon* [the Navy's principal torpedo school] and the Assistant Director of Torpedoes have for the last four or five years been far worse than d___d fools . . . Our torpedoes won't hit, and, when they do hit, produce no more effect than sawdust.' And even three years later, in June 1918, a writer was saying in an Admiralty document, 'Hitting with torpedoes is very chancy work.'

Fisher pointed out that his submarine dreadnought could carry far more 850-pound shells than torpedoes. His faith in the scheme was such that he offered, as he put it later, 'to humiliate myself' by returning to the Admiralty as Third Sea Lord for six months to see the project through. The submarine dreadnought, he declared, would 'end the war'. But Balfour side-stepped the whole proposal.

Not to be outdone, Fisher made use of his protégé in charge of submarines, Commodore Hall. In September and October of 1915 Hall presented to the Admiralty's Submarine Development Committee the arguments in favour of arming submarines with a 12-inch gun, thus:

> No case is known of a ship-of-war being torpedoed when under way at a range outside 1,000 yards. The result is that opportunities of inflicting damage on the enemy have very often been missed, even though the submarine has been brought unobserved within a mile of them . . . The method of using the gun would be as follows: On sighting a surface ship the submarine would proceed as for torpedo attack; should this not be possible

because of a zigzag alteration, or should the torpedo miss or be dodged, the submarine would break the surface within about a mile of the enemy and use the gun [which would have a maximum movement vertically and horizontally of twenty degrees].

The gun casing and the conning-tower only would appear above the water for not longer than forty-five seconds. The facts that the gun could only be reloaded on the surface and that, as Hall concluded in his report, it was 'difficult to lay down the submarine's rôle definitely', were not considered to be of major importance. The final telling argument which Fisher had put to Hall and which he in turn put to the Submarine Development Committee was that the Germans were probably already planning big gun submarines and 'unless something is done towards getting a design ready, we may find ourselves thus placed at a disadvantage'.

Working with Commodore Hall, the Director of Naval Construction quickly produced a design for a submarine dreadnought utilising the keel and some of the general outline of the K boat, but reverting to diesel engines for surface power. In February of 1916 the Admiralty placed an order for one of these boats with Vickers. The firm was to use the keel of K18, but the new boat was to be known ultimately as M1. Officially it was described as a monitor submarine. 'The term is used', Commodore Hall said, 'for want of a better one.' In the ensuing months of 1916 the keels of K19 at Vickers, and K20 and K21 at Armstrong Whitworth, were all turned over to use in M boats.

Strict secrecy covered the project. At Vickers' yard only a few key men knew that K18 would emerge in a different guise. The Sea Lords and the flag officers, like Lord Fisher, saw the monitor submarine as a terrible weapon. Indeed, the more they thought about it, the more anxious they became. In the hands of the Hun a similar boat might cause unprecedented havoc among British ships. Even Fisher himself, having at last got his way about his submarine dreadnought, began to have second thoughts. The delay since he had put the idea forward irked him. In it he found an excuse for a change of mind. No sooner had the Admiralty placed the first order with Vickers than he wrote to Jellicoe:

There are Germans or pro-Germans very closely connected with our affairs, and it is astonishing and marvellous how the Germans spy and how utterly ignorant we are as to German naval doings! Suppose the Germans have constructed such a type [of monitor submarine]. Why not? What about your safety, the safety of the Grand Fleet at Scapa Flow?

111

This aspect of the M boat project weighed heavily on the minds of the Sea Lords. It no longer seemed so important 'to keep abreast of what appeared to be an expected development', one of the justifications used at the planning stage. Before long all work on K18, alias M1, was stopped. Tarpaulins were draped over her. The plans were hidden. Someone had decided that there was a chance that the Germans had not thought of the idea, and it was better to deny the boat to the Navy than to let the enemy have a sight of her.

A year passed before work began on her again, and it was not until the spring of 1918 that she went into commission. There was much shipyard and lower-rank criticism of the design. To mount a gun weighing sixty tons taken from a battleship on to a submarine seemed to many people madness. They prophesied that she would capsize in a sea-way, and that if the crew ever managed to fire the gun the recoil would drive her backwards, and probably sink her. None of these catastrophes occurred. On her trials she achieved 15 knots on the surface and 10 knots underwater. She dived in thirty seconds with complete docility. The gun proved most reliable, maintaining a high level of accuracy and firing after being loaded for a week during which the submarine was often at a depth of 100 feet for several hours. Submariners nicknamed the new M class 'mutton boats', because the gun and its turret resembled a leg of mutton. The evolution in which the gun was fired came to be called the dip-chick.

When at last M1 was ready for action in June 1918 some people felt that too much time, effort and money had gone into the creation of a warship with a fire-power of one 850-pound shell. Whatever the Admiralty had once thought of M1's potentialities, it did not make use of them now: instead of fighting through the last months of the war along the German North Sea coast, she was sent to the Mediterranean, where she had no contact with the enemy at all.

Confused but dogmatic thinking had created the M class; and confused but dogmatic thinking kept the K class alive. The Admiralty ordered the six new K boats, not only in the face of two years' practical experience which condemned both the seaworthiness and the fighting qualities of the class, but without reference to the opinions of the men who had to man them. Had the Admiralty asked them, Leir, Layton, Gravener, de Burgh, Harbottle and Vaughan Jones could have delivered some telling criticisms of both the K boats and the concept of fleet submarines.

By mid-1918 the class had a frightening reputation. Naval security was such that secrets leaked to the ranks in exaggerated form. Bad as it was, the Battle of May Island achieved far worse dimensions in the accounts of it told on the mess-decks. This was bound to happen when both naval and military high commands followed a policy of telling the men as little as possible about setbacks and losses. But the security organisation could claim some credit for hiding the truth, because for years after the accident even official accounts were inaccurate. An Admiralty paper entitled *British Submarine Organisation in the 1914–18 War* says: 'The only occasion on which it was attempted to use submarines in conjunction with the fleet was in November 1917, when the K21 was rammed by the K40.' No submarines then in service bore those numbers.

Before 1924 only volunteers manned British submarines, but in 1918 few were eager to serve in the K class. The late Admiral Sir Max Horton, then a distinguished submarine commander, told Commodore Hall that he would prefer not to be posted to a K boat. In the early twenties he commanded a K-class flotilla from the cruiser escort, but never served in the submarines. Many ratings tried to avoid serving in them but with less success.

Soon after the end of the war the antipathy to the K boats became so pronounced that the Naval Society addressed its officer-members on the subject in these chiding terms:

Service in K boats is usually avoided for the rather vague reason that K boats are no good; an entirely mistaken idea, as the writer attempts to show in this essay.

The K boats were designed when the need for submarines capable of working with the battle fleet was first realised, and were laid down early in 1916. The appreciations of the tactics at Jutland showed how imperative it was to have fleet submarines.

The first and principal essential required for this work is sufficient speed to be able to keep the speed of the fleet in most weathers; and to get this, quick-diving qualities had to be sacrificed in the same way that armour and guns were sacrificed in battle-cruisers. Remembering that speed is all important, it is seen that the K boats' design is highly successful, a speed of twenty-four knots being obtained, which is sufficient to allow for twenty knots being kept up in moderate weather.

Critics who maintain that in bad weather the speed must be reduced to a crawl have scarcely studied the question from a large enough standpoint.

In a case of urgency a K boat can keep up a speed of fifteen to twenty knots in weather that would force destroyers to reduce to fifteen knots or break up; admittedly, damage to the bridge and superstructure must be expected, and the stokers in the boiler-room would suffer severe discomfort from water pouring down the air intakes and funnels, sometimes extinguishing the fires (which can very quickly be relighted), but the main point is that the half-inch hull will not suffer from any amount of over-driving in bad weather like the thin plating of a destroyer; so unless the C-in-C was willing to leave his destroyers he would never have to outpace his K boats.

(Note – It is quite usual for stokers to go on watch in the boiler-room wearing oilskins, sou'westers and sea boots.)

Having this speed makes it possible for K boats to get into an attacking position before the battleship duel begins – no other submarines could do this; those that left harbour at the same time as the fleet would not arrive till the action was over and those already on patrol near enough to see the enemy would not have sufficient speed to place themselves in an attacking position unless by chance they were already there.

Given the necessary speed, the other essentials are as large a number of torpedo tubes as possible (which was fulfilled by building four bow and four beam), and a good tactician as Captain (S) for the flotilla leader in a light cruiser. (During the war the battle fleet submarine flotilla was fortunate in having an exceptionally able tactician as Captain (S).)

In the battle formation of the Grand Fleet [in exercises], during the war, the K boats were stationed 10 miles ahead of the main battle squadrons with various light forces spread out ahead of them to a distance of about 25 miles.

On the screening force sighting the enemy and reporting by W/T, the Captain (S) had to manoeuvre to place his flotilla ahead of the probable course of the enemy battle fleet, and, if possible, slightly on the side farthest from our own heavy ships. When in position the boats were detached in pairs to act independently; generally at least three pairs could be counted on as being present, the distance between them varying according to the circumstances to ensure that two pairs got in their attack even if the enemy made a considerable alteration in course.

The boats of a pair then separated to about one mile, by previous arrangement, to avoid the chances of underwater collision, and prepared for diving. When the leading enemy ships were about four miles off the boats would dive, taking at most five minutes, as they would be already trimmed down; and it must be remembered that the conning tower, end on, is very difficult to see even in calm weather at two miles, and in action the firing of our light forces would probably distract the attention of enemy look-outs sufficient to ensure the K boats being unobserved.

After diving the range of action is very much restricted and unless the Captain (S) had slipped the boats in the correct positions the enemy would pass out of range of the boats, which can only proceed at seven knots when submerged.

Should the boats be in the correct position, the action radius of seven knots for about one hour would be more than sufficient, as the high speed would not be much required, and long before the hour had elapsed the action would have passed over the horizon.

Unless the enemy turned 16 points shortly after the K boats dived, they must pass close to them, or else turn away towards our own battle fleet, either procedure suiting the C-in-C whose tactics would be formed accordingly.

Taking the first case of proceeding on the same course or turning slightly away from our battle fleet; the K boats would find themselves in an ideal attacking position from where their experienced captains could not fail to obtain at least 60 per cent of hits and probably would obtain 90 per cent.

Imagine 29 torpedoes hitting before the gun duel had even begun!

If the enemy turned towards our battle fleet, or turned 16 points when 4,000 yards away, the submarines could still fire 'browning' salvoes of torpedoes set for 19 knots, of which, by the laws of chance, at least 25 per cent would hit, and several ships would probably be damaged enough to be unable to keep in line.

Even if the submarines were sighted during their attack only capital ships could ram them if at periscope depth, and in the unlikely event of destroyers carrying depth charges during a fleet action, it seems improbable that that many boats would be sunk before they had time to fire their torpedoes.

The time taken to reload the tubes makes it unlikely that many 'second shots' could be fired before the enemy passed out of range; the boats would then, after attacking stragglers, concentrate on a pre-arranged line off the enemy coast to intercept returning ships.

Critics also deride the usefulness of K boats on patrol, forgetting that to be present in a fleet action is the primary cause of their existence – patrols were a secondary consideration introduced chiefly for exercising the boats, which were found to suffer from numerous minor breakdowns after too long a period in harbour, and from this point of view patrols were most beneficial, the average number of effective boats being nearly doubled after a few weeks of patrols. The duty of a K boat on patrol is rather different to any other submarine on lookout duty.

Should an enemy vessel be sighted the K boat reports at once, and probably has finished her signal and 'trimmed down' before she is seen herself; and can then get to periscope depth in four minutes, her external hull being underwater in less than two minutes; the chance of a shell damaging her inner hull when in this position is extremely remote, especially at short range when shells would burst, or ricochet, on the water or her outer hull. The superstructure might be shot to pieces without doing more damage than flooding the conning tower and lower funnels, which could easily be adjusted for in the trim.

The objections to the discomfort of living on the boat, and being 'one of a crowd' instead of having a little action alone, and consequently reaping all the credit, are both obvious and true; but the writer hopes this essay will save K boats from a little of the unmerited ridicule heaped on them by so many submarine officers who, in many cases, have never seen one, and have no conception of their duties and tactics in action.

To sum up in brief the use of K boats, it may be said that: As surface ships, they can get to the scene of action and choose their attacking position, after which they have, except for a small difference of speed, the same chance of making a successful attack as any other submarine in the same position.

Similar attempts to whitewash the class, often in a manner little short of naïve, appeared in other documents published by the Admiralty. In a technical history of the war at sea a section dealing with Submarine Administration, Training and Construction declared:

The K class stands by itself. No other nation is building similar boats and our inception of them shows that our lead in design is very great. They showed that we could confidently produce a successful boat of any size and specification asked for, and that we have long passed the stage of experimental construction. The K boats were required to steam to 23 knots, to dive in five minutes, to dive for six hours, and to be seaworthy on the high seas.

Their performance is:
Good diving time, 4 mins15 secs. (3 mins 25 secs. In K8 on one occasion – unofficial checking.)
Surface speed 24.2 knots. (Over 72 miles in K12 checked by two ships.)
Submerged endurance, about 10 hours in calm weather.
Sea-keeping capacity: In September 1918 two K boats overtook the Grand Fleet which was hove-to in a heavy N.W. gale by the North Dogger Bank.

The document ignored the many occasions on which K flotillas had to drop out of exercises because of water flooding down the funnels, but it did go on to say that 'those figures show the best performances' and that 'in the gale mentioned, several K boats were strained and damaged'. Under a heading dealing with fleet submarines, it reported that the K boats 'are the largest submarines in the world, being 50 feet longer than the German so-called cruisers of 'U139' type'. This reference to the long-range cruising U-boats overlooked one highly pertinent fact. The end of the war and the surrender of the High Seas Fleet had at last exposed as false all stories and theories which had caused the K class to be rushed into production. The German Navy had built no high-speed U-boats. It had built no fleet submarines. Nor had it planned any.

CHAPTER SEVEN

A LETHAL SEESAW

A hen's egg is strong and so is an ostrich egg, but if the shell of the ostrich egg was as thin as the shell of the hen's egg it would be very weak indeed; in the same way a 'K' boat is structurally weaker to resist deep pressures than is an 'E' boat . . . – Submarine Administration, Training and Construction, published by the Technical History Section of the Admiralty, 1921.

I think we realised that we were being expected to do things with our K boats after the war that were beyond their capability; instead of being sulky and unwilling about it, there arose rather a 'devil-may-care' attitude of 'We'll do it – or bust.' – Commander Arthur Ashworth, R.N. (retd.), in a letter, November 1959.

In the Victory Cruise made by units of the Grand Fleet in June 1919, the K boats appeared in force. Unsuspecting members of the public in the coastal towns of Britain might reasonably have supposed that the impressive steam submarines had played a conspicuous rôle in the war.

Their future rôle at this time seemed uncertain. The Grand Fleet was being dispersed, and the Atlantic Fleet re-formed. K3 had gone to the scrapheap, and K7 was soon to be put up for sale. Admiral Sir Reginald Hall, M.P., the wartime director of Naval Intelligence, wrote to the construction department of the Admiralty asking whether K boats were suitable for conversion to coastal cargo steamers. The idea received the fullest consideration, but was rejected because it would call for a very low sale price, and extensive alterations to the craft.

If as a result of these developments any members of the Submarine Service hoped that they would soon see the last of the K class they were to be confounded in October 1919 by the appointment of Admiral Sir David Beatty as First Sea Lord, a position he was to hold for the unprecedented period of eight years. Beatty was known to be of the opinion that the new warship of the future would be a submersible battle-cruiser. It was fitting that within a month of his promotion a second M boat went into commission. At about the same time seven

117

K boats were formed into the 1st Submarine Flotilla of the Atlantic Fleet.

At last Admiralty post-war policy was clarified. For the Navy as a whole, much hard work was prescribed as an antidote to any peacetime staleness among the officers and men. As for the K class, the Submarine Service would take advantage of the lead it held in the design of large submarines. Let the other navies of the world ponder and dither over the building of fleet submarines and submersible battle-cruisers: in the meantime, the 1st Submarine Flotilla would gain valuable ocean-going experience, taking part in a full programme of all-weather exercises with the Atlantic Fleet. The other five K boats would engage in experimental work, including high-speed trials and torpedo testing.

In the twelve months after the armistice the steam submarines lost none of their propensity for getting into trouble. Twice in one month K15 dived out of control in the North Sea and struck the bottom. K8 caught fire at Chatham while refitting. K14 was all but lost when a boiler explosion forced open the mushroom ventilators as she was diving. The boiler-room flooded and only swift action in the control and engine-rooms brought the submarine safely to the surface. No sooner had she refitted than she suffered another explosion and fire, this time in her batteries.

After the formation of the 1st Flotilla the K boats logged hundreds of sea hours in the deep waters of the Atlantic without serious mishap. The Atlantic Fleet worked hard in the autumn of 1919, and in the spring and summer of 1920 the Fleet visited Arosa Bay, Gibraltar, Majorca and Algiers, but only at Algiers were the crews allowed a few days' respite. This was the first peacetime visit by the Navy to a foreign port since before the war and it was outstanding for the number of parties, dances, *vins d'honneur* and other less sophisticated social gatherings. When the party ended, Commander John Hutchings, the senior submarine officer commanding K5, doubtless brimming with *joie de vivre*, led the 1st Flotilla out of Algiers harbour at 18 knots.

On the way home the submarines took a drubbing from a strong south-westerly wind and following sea. The last night coming up the Channel was full of peril. Two boats developed the old fuel feed trouble known as losing suction and came to an unexpected halt. But no collisions occurred, and the next morning the boats scattered to their various home ports for Easter leave.

When the crews returned, K5 had a new commander, Lieutenant-Commander John Austin Gaimes, D.S.O. A most experienced submariner, Jackie Gaimes had been with the flotilla, serving in its escort cruiser, *Inconstant,* for six months. During the war he had won a considerable reputation as captain of a mine-laying E-boat working out of Harwich. Now thirty-three, he was soon to be initiated into the fickle ways of the K class. Early that summer, during exercises in Largo Bay, in the Firth of Forth, K5 got out of control while diving, and buried her bows in the muddy bottom of the estuary. For ten minutes she lay at an angle of forty-five degrees with her depth gauges indicating 120 feet and her stern sticking out of the water. Gaimes put the engines astern but the whirring bronze propellers, glinting in the sun, succeeded only in attracting the attention of *Inconstant.* Presently the captain blew the forward external ballast tanks and K5 surfaced. A board of inquiry failed to explain the mishap.

In July the 1st Flotilla, now gathered at Scapa Flow, sailed south to join the Atlantic Fleet in Tor Bay. The submarines called on the way at Milford Haven and were then ordered to sea hurriedly at night. As K5 steamed down the harbour she crashed into an obsolete destroyer in tow. A tug had anchored without pulling the destroyer alongside her. The damage to both vessels was superficial and above their water-lines but the swan bows of the submarine were noticeably crumpled. Gaimes pressed on to Tor Bay and arrived twenty-four hours ahead of the surface ships, determined to hide all traces of the collision until he could be sure his report had reached the Commander-in-Chief. Using wire, glue and canvas, the crew built a dummy bow which for three days fooled the Commander-in-Chief as he passed by in his barge not fifty yards away. Only on the fourth day, when the flotilla was ordered to sea for diving exercises, was the camouflage uncovered; by then Gaimes's official report had reached the flagship.

The end of the year found K5 at Chatham completing a refit. Meanwhile on 12 December the officer commanding the K boats in reserve at Rosyth dockyard received from the Admiralty a telegram which read: 'K2, K10, K16 to be paid off for disposal and sold.'

A series of articles on the future of the submarine appearing in the August 1920 issue of the *Naval Review* aroused much discussion among submarine officers that winter. All the writers showed a continuing enthusiasm for fleet submarines. 'It is difficult to see how our fleet submarine tactics can be improved in principle', said one. The same writer mentioned 'the British K Class, a wonderfully successful experiment considering how long ago they were designed'. Another writer emphasised the need for fleet submarines, but added that the K class, 'having been designed essentially for operations in the North Sea . . . cannot be said to meet modern requirements'. Two of the articles acknowledged that the sea-keeping qualities of the K boats were poor. These last opinions, however, did nothing to deter the Admiralty from using the K flotillas with the Atlantic Fleet.

During K5's refit a high proportion of the officers and crew were relieved. Of the officers only Gaimes remained. His Number One, Lieutenant Arthur Ashworth, was replaced by Lieutenant Frederick W. F. Cuddeford from K11. None of the other new officers had K boat experience.

Fresh from the Christmas leave, K5 left Chatham in early January to join K9 at Portsmouth. On 14 January the two submarines sailed once more to join the Atlantic Fleet in Tor Bay. K5 called in at Portland on the way to pick up a spare captain, Lieutenant-Commander Reginald Darke. On K9, a hitch occurred off St Alban's Head. As a matter of routine after spending a month in the dockyard, the captain ordered a dive to check the trim of the boat. With the first of the tanks flooding, the red light signalling 'Engine-room shut' failed to shine in the control-room. The captain closed the vents, broke off the dive and telephoned the engine-room. Expletives coloured the explanation that the boiler-room air intakes would not fully close. The submarine regained her surface trim and an officer went on deck to examine the funnel superstructure. Someone had stowed a heaving-line carelessly and it had jammed under one of the mushroom ventilators.

At Tor Bay K5 and K9 anchored near K8, K15 and K22 on the northern edge of a giant armada. The fleet was scheduled to sail for Spain the next morning, carrying out exercises under war conditions on the way. But during the night a gale blew up and pinned the ships in the bay. For three days they yawed on their anchor cables, largely hidden from one-another and the shore by the high, spraying seas. With Torquay breakwater under their lee, the K boats kept an anxious anchor watch.

On 20 January the gale moderated and the fleet sailed, dividing itself into two opposing forces named Red and Blue. At the head of one force, *Inconstant* disposed her K boats in line formations behind her, K5 and K9 on her starboard quarter, K22, K15 and K8 on the port. All that day and through the night the flotilla pushed south-westward towards a prearranged battle zone. It was a black moonless night, and with a heavy swell still running and each submarine allowed to show only a dimmed and shaded sternlight they kept station with difficulty. In the early morning the officer of the watch on K9 lost sight of K5. He was about to increase speed to catch up with her when her stern loomed into view and came rapidly nearer. The officer on K9 took evasive action while his signalman picked out a winking message from K5: 'O.O.W. to ditto. Sorry. Lost suction.'

In mid-morning the mock battle began. *Inconstant* made a sighting ahead and signalled to the submarines to spread out ready to attack. Over the western horizon the masts of the opposition's cruiser screen hove into view. *Inconstant* doubled back along her course as if she were fleeing. The submarines lowered their wireless masts and uncovered their periscope wells. On K5 a signalman flagged an underwater course for each of the other boats, followed by the command: 'Dive.' K5 herself went down first. The opposition cruisers were moving at high speed and if the submarines were to make a surprise attack they had to get out of sight fast.

K9 had trouble getting under. With some ten feet of her conning-tower above the surface, she would go down no farther. The captain examined the telemotor panel, but all sixteen vents on the external ballast tanks were properly open. To confirm the fact, all the tanks were reported full. But she would not dive.

'What the hell's the matter, Number One?' the captain asked.

On the coxswain's spirit-level the bubble was forward: she was still light by the bows.

Acting on this unaccountable evidence, the captain said, 'Flood B.' B was an internal tank of 18 tons capacity under the wardroom. As it filled the depth gauges moved a couple of feet, then stopped again. Eight feet of conning-tower remained above the surface. With one eye on the periscope, watching the advancing cruisers, the captain fumed at the submarine's stubbornness. Any minute now the opposition look-outs would spot him. At that moment the first lieutenant vaguely saw in his mind's eye the bows of the submarine as they appeared when he left the bridge: in the image the vents were not open. To confirm his hunch, he squinted through the forward periscope and there, sure enough, were the two manhole covers, closed tight.

The officer pointed at the man on the control panel and snapped, 'Bow vents.' The operating lever was in the open position, but two safety stop-valves on each side of the lever had been overlooked when K9 put to sea. The bows of the boat were full of air, acting like a balloon.

The seaman reached to open the valves, but the officer grabbed his wrist. B tank had to be emptied first. A minute later, with everything in order K9 dived in perfect trim to periscope depth. In the control-room the Number One silently reflected on what might have happened if the erring seaman had quietly opened the bow vents with B tank still full.

During the time that K9 had been struggling to get under water the jinx-ridden K22 had been struggling to return to the surface. On diving she had taken on an alarming bow-down angle, and her captain,

Commander Allan Poland, knew enough about K boats to take no chances. He ordered full astern on both engines and all tanks to be blown at full pressure. The submarine surfaced, abandoned the attack and theoretically put herself out of action.

An hour or so later the K flotilla had finished its part in the battle, and the submarines began to reappear at widely scattered points and to report their positions by radio to *Inconstant*. The cruiser asked them in turn if they could see K5. The answer in every case was no. It was just after midday.

Down the afternoon the cruiser and the submarines hung about, waiting for K5, calling up the other ships of the fleet to ask whether they had seen or heard anything of her. About an hour before dusk the flotilla returned to the position where the K boats had dived. Calculations by dead reckoning after an underwater exercise could not be highly reliable, but eventually the men on watch saw ahead an area of calmed water about a mile square, and this led them exactly to the spot where K5 had gone down. They could smell the oil several minutes before the submarines slithered into it. In the thick of the oil slick two pieces of timber floated, splintered at the ends. K9 picked them up. Their sides were painted in red with consecutive numbers picked out in white at eighteen-inch intervals. Every K-boat man knew what they were: beams from the battery cover of a K boat. The movable floorboards in the control-room rested on these beams. The white numbers indicated the different cells of the battery.

That evening the Commander-in-Chief of the Atlantic Fleet, Sir Charles Madden, telegraphed the Admiralty:

> Regret to report loss of submarine K5 with entire crew while diving to attack battle-cruisers during tactical exercise in about Latitude 49 N Longitude 9 West at about 11.30 today Thursday 20 January. Cause not known. Patches of oil and wreckage have been located. It is hoped to ascertain definitely the nature of the wreckage at daylight. H.M.S. Inconstant and destroyers are on spot. Am proceeding Arosa Bay in Queen Elizabeth with Second and Fourth destroyer flotillas, H.M.S. Inconstant and First Submarine Flotilla to hold enquiry. Remainder of Atlantic Fleet will proceed on Spring Cruise as already arranged.

A subsequent telegram pinpointed the position of the accident as Latitude 48° 51½'N. Longitude 9° 5'W., which is about 120 miles west-south-west of the Scilly Islands. The telegram ended: 'List of officers and men is in (H.M.S.) *Pandora* at Portland.' At first the spare captain, Lieutenant-Commander Darke, was included among the missing, presumed dead, but it was then discovered that he had left K5 while the fleet was anchored in Tor Bay.

The next morning one of the research ships picked up the lid of the torpedo gunners' mate's ditty box. And that was all. The sea gave up no further trace of the 339-foot submarine. She had disappeared at a point where the bed of the Atlantic drops prodigiously. She might be lying in six hundred feet of water or twelve thousand feet. Wherever she was, her crew of six officers and fifty-one men lay with her. As night closed in on 21 January the cruiser *Inconstant* and the four remaining K boats made their way forlornly south towards Arosa Bay.

The inquiry achieved little. The three items of evidence showed that the submarine had broken up. It could have happened in three ways. She might have exploded; she might have broken in half; or, as was most likely, she might have got out of control, dived too deep, and collapsed when the pressure became too great.

The pieces of wreckage all came from the control-room, indicating that the breakdown had occurred there. The weakest point in the pressure hull of a K boat was in the roof of the control-room where its smooth lines were interrupted by a dome jutting into the conning-tower. Under excessive pressure the dome would almost certainly have caved in first.

The loss of K5 unleashed much criticism of the Admiralty's policy with the K class. The public was shocked and might have been more so if it had known the history of the class. The views of the submariners themselves found expression in the columns of *The Times* in this article, written by Rear-Admiral (retd.) Sydney Hall, who had commanded the Submarine Service during the War:

> K class submarines were designed solely for action with the Grand Fleet in the North Sea. They are the largest and fastest submarines in existence, certainly by far the most complicated, and they need an exceptionally well-trained crew.
>
> It is not known what rapidity of diving was being demanded by the operation orders, but it seems certain that the first lieutenant, on whom would fall the chief duty of supervision below, was recently appointed, and that many of the crew were also newly-joined . . .
>
> The accident is deplorable in the loss of so many gallant officers and men, and it is not clear why the K class should be taken for cruises in the Atlantic in the winter. The vessels may with accuracy be described as 'freak' submarines, built entirely for the peculiar conditions of the last war. The high surface speed necessitates great length, and the further complication of steam demands very large openings for funnels and air intakes to the boiler-rooms. These have always been a source

of great anxiety in bad weather or in rapid diving . . .

Presumably these vessels are kept in commission in order to perfect the conduct of such submarines in a fleet battle, but it appears to be a very questionable policy, since the K class will be obsolete long before such a battle can take place. They were designed solely for the North Sea, and have not the qualifications nor the sea endurance to accompany a battle fleet under war conditions except in home waters.

The keenness of all submarine officers is well known. It is to be hoped that this has not been overstrained from a lack of understanding of the delicacy of this very special type of submarine, with the result of the vessels' being employed on work for which they were never intended, and for which they would be highly dangerous if the personnel were not thoroughly trained . . .

It has always been recognised that owing to their size and complications the K class cannot dive as rapidly as smaller submarines. For work with the fleet this was no disadvantage, since they could always expect to get good warning; but a highly trained crew, thoroughly familiar with every detail of the vessel, is required. With such conditions the K boats could dive from twenty knots on the surface in about four minutes, but with anything but a perfectly trained crew, any attempt to do this would be highly dangerous in deep water. With water entering the tanks at two hundred tons a minute, the vessel might easily be trimmed to such an extent that the slightest hitch in getting the compressed air to act would take the vessel too deep for recovery. It will easily be understood that as the vessel now weights over two and a half thousand tons and has way on her, the downward momentum may be considerable. If there is much sea or swell it may be imperative to give her some negative buoyancy to get her away from the surface, and though the compressed air will blow one or two tanks rapidly there is often considerable delay in checking the vessel's downward motion. This is especially the case if the tank or tanks to which the air is admitted are not quite full and the vessel is already getting deep. The air has first of all to raise the pressure in the whole of the empty portion of the tank. During this time the water is still entering and rising in pressure, and only when the air pressure exceeds this and commences to drive the water out will buoyancy begin to be gained. Even then it will be an appreciable time before the vessel is checked and then begins to rise . . .

It will be readily understood that diving a vessel of this size and intricacy is a delicate operation, demanding the complete knowledge of his duty from every member of her crew and a perfect system of drill and control from the central compartment before rapid diving can be safely undertaken.

The Admiralty made no public comment on the disaster other than to express its deep regret, but it ordered the fitting of high-pressure air systems to the forward external ballast tanks on all K boats. On 25 January K2 was reprieved from the scrapheap: she would live to dive another day as the replacement for K5 in the 1st Flotilla.

Chapter Eight

... And Then There Were Seven

Though I descend to the depths I arise more beautiful. – Motto on K15.

On a summer night five months after the disappearance of K5 her sister-ship, K15, lay alongside the light cruiser *Canterbury* in the tidal basin at Portsmouth. It had been a scorching day but it was much cooler now. Most of the crew of the submarine – and this included her captain, Commander George Fagan Bradshaw, D.S.O. – were on leave, and only a few were on board. Most of them were asleep, or trying to sleep, when the watch-keeper on his rounds discovered that K15 was sinking. The water was creeping up her sides and over her decks. Most of the stern was already awash. The watch-keeper hurled himself down the conning-tower and roused the others. Just in time they scrambled on to the *Canterbury*. Beneath them the submarine slowly submerged herself amid streams of phosphorescent bubbles.

At low tide the next morning her funnels and the top of her conning-tower broke the surface. Lying near the mouth of the tidal basin, she presented a considerable hazard. Divers went down at once. They found that most of the vents on the external ballast tanks were leaking. The immediate cause of the accident was almost certainly the hot weather of the previous day. The oil in the hydraulic system which closed the vents airtight had expanded and overflowed, then contracted in the cool of the evening. The system was not topped up, and the contraction caused a drop in the oil pressure sufficient to slacken the vents and allow air to escape. As the air pressure in the tanks dropped the sea-water rose.

The salvage work began at once. Vaughan Jones, the first man to command K15, was called in to give advice. The job would have been relatively simple had all the watertight doors, hatches and intakes been closed in the pressure hull. But a manhole door on the cable locker had been left open, and most of the watertight doors separating

126

the submarine's compartments were open. As a result, she was flooded from end to end. Even so, the salvage work ought to have been straightforward with the conning-tower hatch well clear of the water at low tide. But the previous day dockyard workers had been carrying out some minor refitting and had drilled a hole one-inch wide through the pressure hull into the control-room. From outside the boat the divers tried in vain to plug the hole. Eventually, they had to tackle the salvage problem through the funnels, closing one and fitting an extension to the other so that it was clear of the water at all states of the tide. Entering the submarine through this funnel, they pumped out the compartments. The salvage team worked sixteen hours a day, and, with only one rest day, brought K15 to the surface thirteen days after she had sunk. Soon afterwards a tug took her to the mud flats near Whale Island. There she lay for months. One day, looking at the miserable wreck, Vaughan Jones remembered the inscribed brass plate he had fitted in her when he commissioned her in 1918. He asked the chief engine-room artificer who had served with him on the boat to get the plate for him as a souvenir. But someone had been there before him and relieved the boat of its now incongruous motto. From her last descent to the depths she had arisen anything but more beautiful. In the end the breakers bought her.

CHAPTER NINE

LAST FLING

It is an extraordinary fact that even after the war was over and the lesson supposedly learnt, one more of these boats was built. – H.M. Submarines, by Lieutenant-Commander P.K. Kemp, R.N.

Throughout the first half of the 1920s the Admiralty maintained its fleet submarine strength. At Chatham in 1921 work began again on a new K boat. She was K26, the only boat in the last batch of six ordered in July 1918 to be built so far. Launched from the Vickers yard at Barrow in 1919, she had gone under tow to Chatham for fitting out, but the work had been delayed. Now she was to be completed with extensive modifications, including an increased range, armament and displacement, and improved systems for closing the funnels and air intakes, for feeding the oil into the furnaces and for flowing the ballast tanks. Much was expected of K26. If all went well with her she would head a new class which would replace the original K boats. In the meantime the big-gun 'mutton boat', M3, which had originally been laid down as K20, was commissioned at Portsmouth and joined the 1st flotilla of the Atlantic Fleet as a replacement for K15. Not long afterwards M1 and M2 took the places of K8 and K9, both of which went into the reserve.

The fleet submarine policy was pursued in the face of further disasters which pointed to the inadvisability of working submarines closely with surface ships. As well as the 1st Flotilla of K and M boats, the Atlantic Fleet employed two flotillas of the smaller H and L class submarines. Though not strictly fleet submarines, they took part in fleet exercises and manoeuvres. On 23 March, 1922, the destroyer *Versatile* rammed and sank H42, killing twenty-six men, during exercises off Europa Point, Gibraltar. The same year H.M.S. *Vancouver* rammed H24 when she was submerged during exercises, and badly damaged the conning-tower but did not breach the pressure hull. No one died. On 10 January, 1924, the battleship *Resolution* rammed and sank L24 off Portland Bill. Again the accident occurred during exercises and while the submarine was under water. Forty-three submariners died.

As for the remaining K boats in service, Navy dockyards had fitted them in quick rotation with a newly designed high-pressure system for blowing the forward external ballast tanks. K22 had it installed first, and off Campbeltown, on the west coast of Scotland, gave an unexpectedly impressive demonstration to senior officers of the Atlantic Fleet who watched from the cruiser *Norfolk*. True to form, K22's performance was near-disastrous: she dived with her funnels raised. With water cascading into the boiler-room, the tanks were blown with the new system and she thumped back to the surface.

K6 had the high-pressure device fitted at Chatham, then sailed north for Invergordon. On the way up the east coast she ran into a gale which whipped up heavy confused head seas. Pitching severely, the submarine blundered into the waves, rising on to the crests with thirty feet of her bows overhanging the troughs. As the bows pounded down and into the next wave, they seemed to twist under the strain. A hurried examination of the forward compartments showed that a number of rivets in the pressure hull were leaking. The captain eased his speed to eight knots and reach Invergordon safely. There, a detailed inspection confirmed that the bows of the boat had been working. The fault was attributed to a weakness stemming from the submarine's collision with K4 six years earlier. In calmer conditions she returned to Chatham for repairs.

At the same yard two months later, K26 claimed her first victims while she was being prepared for trials. Faulty valves in the boiler-room caused a blow-back of steam which scalded two men to death. *The Engineer* commented: 'It would appear . . . that she is not free from the disabilities . . . of the other units of her class.'

With the commissioning of K26 in 1923, six K boats were in service and two in the reserve. Later in the year the 1st Flotilla was temporarily weakened when K2 and K12 collided while leaving Portland Harbour in the early hours of a morning. K2 carved a huge hole in K12's forward casing and bent her own stem, but the damage was superficial and both boats were soon in service again.

Though the three Atlantic Fleet submarine flotillas were kept at full strength in the early twenties, the Submarine Service as a whole was cut drastically. At the end of the war it had consisted of sixteen flotillas; by 1924 it had six. Many people in and out of the Navy forecast that the submarine had had its day. Others, including members of the Government, realised that the submarine in another war could form an even more serious threat to Britain's maritime supremacy; and they tried to bring about its abolition by international agreement. A string of disarmament conferences discussed this somewhat naïve answer to the Admiralty's dilemma, but without result.

In Britain the campaign against submarines gained fresh impetus with every new disaster. In the days following 12 November, 1925, it reached a crescendo. On that day the Admiralty issued this statement: 'During exercises early this morning submarine M1 was seen to dive in a position about fifteen miles south of Start Point. She has not been seen since. Every effort is being made to locate her and establish communication.' Sixty-nine men were on board. She was never found. On the tenth day of a most intensive search off the Devon coast, a Swedish ship named *Vidar*, arriving at the Kiel Canal, reported that she had struck a submerged object fifteen miles off Start Point at 7.48 on the morning in question. The helmsman remembered that for a moment the ship had refused to answer the helm. Both the captain and the first officer thought they had struck an old or dummy mine. But an examination in dry dock at Kiel showed that the lower part of *Vidar's* stem was bent, her plates were buckled, and on the port side of her bottom were traces of grey-green paint which was chemically identified with the paint used on M1.

The accident brought a national outcry in Britain, led by the chairman of the committee of Lloyd's, Mr Percy Mackinnon. A report in *The Engineer* of 27 November, 1925, summed up the popular attitude:

> The loss of M1 is the fourth submarine disaster to occur since the war, each involving the total destruction of vessel and crew. One hundred and ninety-three officers and ratings, the very pick of the Navy's manhood, have gone to their death in this tragic fashion. There is a not unnatural tendency on the part of the public to challenge the need for such a heavy toll of life in time of peace. The chairman of Lloyd's has denounced the submarine as 'a deadly machine, which treacherously destroys those in charge of it, and, it is feared, inflicts slow torture as well as death.' His plea for its abolition has been warmly taken up in influential quarters, and the government has already been invited to convoke a conference of the maritime powers to put effect to the suggestion. There is no doubt that the world at large would stand to gain much and lose nothing by the extinction of a naval weapon, which during its relatively brief career, has caused a disproportionate amount of suffering to humanity. Long before the Great War the submarine's victims were numbered by the hundred. During the war its persistent misuse by one of the belligerents covered it with such obloquy that its legitimate achievements have been obscured. Hence it remains a

weapon of sinister associations, and we believe that its formal repudiation by the powers would be hailed with an almost universal chorus of approval.

None of the Great Powers was much moved by this type of loaded sentiment. In the London Navy Treaty of 1930 they could agree only to build no more submarines of a greater surface displacement than 2,000 tons. To Italy, Japan and France, all bent on building large fleets of submarines, this caused no inconvenience whatsoever.

Since the end of the war, these maritime powers had all watched the emergence of the K class and the development of the fleet submarine with some doubt. They had, on the other hand, seen some merit in the large submarine if used for long-range ocean patrols and for minelaying. In 1922 the Japanese naval yard at Kure had laid down an experimental boat named the *Kaigun,* which was in outside appearance almost a replica of the K boat without its funnels.

From this boat stemmed a class of twelve submarines with an operational range of 16,000 miles. At about the same time the Italians launched two classes of large ocean-going submarines; the U.S. Navy produced two cruiser submarines and a giant submersible minelayer of 2,710 tons; and the French, never to be outdone on the high seas, turned out the biggest of them all, the *Surcouf,* of 2,880 tons.

Curiously enough, an element in the United States Navy had campaigned for fleet submarines as far back as 1916, without foreknowledge of the British developments. In *The Proceedings of the United States Naval Institute* that year, Lieutenant (junior grade) F.A. Daubin wrote a paper headed 'The Fleet Submarine'. Daubin said:

> If large seagoing submarines can aid our fleet in locating and defeating the enemy's main fighting forces, and if our harbours will be better protected, then let the keynote of our submarine policy be, The Fleet Submarine . . . Recent war games have pointed to the tremendous value fleet submarines would be in aiding our fleet to defend the coasts . . . The strategical and tactical value of fleet submarines in this case is almost endless . . .
>
> The one great disadvantage of the fleet submarines is that we have none at present in commission . . . Great Britain gained a big ascendancy over the rest of Europe by being the first to build dreadnoughts. Why should not the United States gain a few years over any future enemy by being the first to build fleet submarines?

Daubin's article found some immediate support, but in later issues of U.S.N.I.P. several experts, including a former president of the U.S. Naval War College, decried the idea of fleet submarines. After the war, however, British naval policy influenced the U.S.A. for a time. On 13 July, 1921, the *New York Tribune* declared:

> New types of submarines have been developed, cruiser submarines, fleet submarines and minelaying submarines. We must have these types. Without them our Navy cannot fight a winning war. The worn out ideas of 1916 must give way to the demonstrated naval truths of 1921.

Subsequently the Navy Department strove to use its S class of submarines with the fleet. Smaller, slower but handier than the K boats, the American submarines were no more successful. In 1925 an official report on them stated: 'Experience in manoeuvres indicates that these vessels cannot be considered as a satisfactory type of fleet submarine.'

After the loss of M1 the Navy disbanded the 1st Flotilla, scrapping the remaining K boats and withdrawing M2 and M3 into an Experimental Half-Flotilla at Portsmouth. K26 had gone on an eight months' cruise to Singapore to be tested under tropical conditions, but the report of the captain, Commander George P. Thomson, gave the Admiralty no encouragement to build more K boats. She spent the rest of her days in the Mediterranean, as troublesome to her crews as any of her sister-ships had been. She was scrapped in March 1931.

The last of the K boats had gone, but M2 and M3 remained afloat, and some submariners did not forget that they had the keels and other parts of K19 and K20. According to an old superstition, a change of name never changes the character of a ship for the better, only, if anything, for the worse. In the Experimental Half-Flotilla the two M boats underwent radical structural alterations. M2 was converted to a submersible seaplane carrier. A hangar with a watertight door replaced the 12-inch gun in front of her conning-tower, and a biplane with folding wings was designed to fit into it. A launching catapult ran nearly the entire length of the forecastle. M3 had her big gun removed and was fitted with a minelaying ramp along the deck aft of the conning-tower. Other modifications enabled the submarine to carry a hundred mines and to lay them while on the surface or submerged.

Both boats carried out a number of useful experiments until, on 26 January, 1932, M2 disappeared with sixty men on board. At 10.11 that morning she reported by radio that she was about to dive in West Bay, off Portland. In the afternoon the captain of a Tyneside coasting steamer, which put into Portland to bunker, mentioned in the office of the coaling company that he had seen a large submarine earlier in the day west of Portland Bill. He asked whether submarines often dived stern first. He was told that they never do so, intentionally. Eight days later search ships and divers found M2 lying in 106 feet of water in West Bay, her stern embedded in the sand and her bows well clear of the sea floor. The hangar door, the conning-tower hatch, and the hatch between the hangar and the pressure hull were open. The evidence showed that M2 had sunk in the act of surfacing. Some people said that the hangar doors had been opened too soon. But submarine officers rejected this explanation and offered another. Because M2 was so large, it took nearly fifteen minutes to blow all the main ballast tanks. The accepted method of getting the seaplane airborne as quickly as possible was to open the hangar door as soon as it was well clear of the water, even though some of the stern ballast tanks were not completely empty. In the meantime the stern was held up artificially by the hydroplanes. Submariners suggested a failure in the hydroplanes had caused M2 to slide backwards under the water. Ten months of hazardous salvage operations failed to raise the submarine or to provide a conclusive explanation of the sinking. Soon afterwards the Admiralty scrapped the M3.

For the hardened old K-boat men like Oscar Moth, the coxswain of K13 and of K22, there was no need to search for technical explanations for the loss of M2.

'She was a K boat originally. What more do you need to know?'

POSTSCRIPT

As the motor vehicle has driven the horse from the road, so has the subma-
rine driven the battleship from the sea. – Admiral Sir Percy Scott, in a
letter to *The Times*, 5 June, 1914.

It may be that after all the submarine will prove to be a messenger of peace,
but this is only a prophecy. – Anonymous writer in *The Naval Review*,
February 1914.

In 1954 the United States Navy commissioned the first steam-
driven submarine built in the world since K26. This return to steam
created no public interest at all. The steam turbines, like those of
the K class, gave the new submarine a much higher speed than the
conventional diesel-engined submarine. It was similar, too, in its great
length and displacement. But, unlike the K class, the new submarine
had no oil furnaces, no funnels, no mushroom-shaped air intakes. Heat
from a nuclear reactor raised the steam to drive her turbines both on
the surface and under water. The boat was called *Nautilus.* By the end
of 1962 the U.S. Navy had 26 nuclear submarines in service, and 32
launched (but not commissioned) or under construction.

Britain launched her first nuclear submarine in 1960. Her name,
Dreadnought, implied much. The Navy's previous *Dreadnought,* the fore-
runner of the battleship, had revolutionised the battle fleets at the
beginning of the century. Now the latest *Dreadnought* and her kind have
so changed naval strategy that the battle fleets (with which the K boats
were supposed to sail) no longer exist.

Once scorned, labelled a pirate ship and damned as a floating coffin
for those who sailed in her, the submarine is today the most powerful
single weapon the world has ever seen. As a launching platform for
nuclear rockets, she surpasses the land base because of her mobility
and the jet aeroplane because of her stealth: she can sail submerged
round the world and fire rockets without surfacing.

In an editorial on 6 November, 1961, *The Observer* commented:

POSTSCRIPT

So far as the peace of the world depends on a balance of power or a system of mutual deterrence, the American development of nuclear submarines equipped with nuclear weapons has made that balance more stable than it has ever been before . . . These submarines . . . may be the best guarantee of peace that we can have.

Perhaps for this alone the men who died in those ill-starred freaks in the submarine lineage – the K class – did not die in vain.

APPENDIX A

The K Class

	Builders	Commissioned	Fate
K1	Portsmouth Dockyard	May 1917	Sunk, after collision with K4, 17 November, 1917.
K2	Portsmouth Dockyard	February 1917	Scrapped, 1926.
K3	Vickers Barrow-in-Furness	August 1916	Scrapped, 1920.
K4	Vickers	January 1917	Sunk in collision with K6, 31 January, 1918.
K5	Portsmouth Dockyard	May 1917	Lost on exercises, 20 January, 1921.
K6	Devonport Dockyard	June 1917	Scrapped, 1926.
K7	Devonport Dockyard	July 1917	Scrapped, 1919.
K8	Vickers	March 1917	Scrapped, 1923.
K9	Vickers	May 1917	Scrapped, 1921.
K10	Vickers	June 1917	Scrapped, 1921.
K11	Armstrong Whitworth (Tyneside)	February 1917	Scrapped, 1921.
K12	Armstrong Whitworth	August 1917	Scrapped, 1926.
K13	Fairfield's (Clydeside)	–	Sank on acceptance trials, 29 January, 1917.
K14	Fairfield's (Clydeside)	May 1917	Scrapped, 1925.
K15	Scott's (Clydeside)	May 1918	Sank in Portsmouth Harbour, 25 June, 1921; raised and beached. Scrapped, 1923.
K16	Beardmore's (Clydeside)	May 1918	Scrapped, 1923.
K17	Vickers	March 1917	Sunk in collision with HMS *Fearless*, 31 January, 1918.
K18 became M1	Vickers	April 1918	Sunk in collision with S.S. *Vidar*, 12 November, 1925.
K19 became M2	Vickers	November 1919	Sank on exercises. 26 January, 1932.
K20 became M3	Armstrong Whitworth	1920	Scrapped, 1932.
K21 became M4	Armstrong Whitworth	Cancelled	–
K22 alias K13	Raised and refitted by Fairfield's	October 1916	Scrapped, 1926.
K23 K24 K25	Ordered from Armstrong Whitworth 10 June, 1918	Cancelled	–
K26	Vickers and Chatham Dockyard	May 1923	Scrapped, 1931.
K27 K28	Ordered from Vickers, 10 June, 1918	Cancelled	–

APPENDIX B

Sources

In the following lists of people who have kindly helped me in the research for this book all the naval officers are on the retired list. Where possible I relate the association with K-class submarines. For simplicity, I have omitted awards and decorations.

Correspondence
Admiral of the Fleet The Earl Mountbatten of Burma. *Midshipman K6.*
Admiral of the Fleet Sir Henry Oliver.
Admiral Sir Noel Lawrence. *Captain K2.*
Vice-Admiral P. Ruck Keene.
Rear-Admiral G.P. Thomson. *Captain K26.*
Rear-Admiral A.L.P. Mark-Wardlaw. *Lieutenant K2.*
Captain F.S. Bell. *First Lieutenant K2 and K11.*
Captain R.W. Blacklock. *Captain K22 and K26.*
Captain C. Coltar. *Captain K2.*
Captain H.B. Crane. *First Lieutenant K5.*
Captain J. Creswell. *First Lieutenant K15.*
Captain W.R.D. Crowther. *Captain K6.*
Captain W.E.C. Davy.
Captain R.C.S. Garwood. *Lieutenant K12.*
Captain A.C. Hemsley. *Naval Secretary to Commodore (Submarines),* 1915-19.
Captain J.F. Hutchings. *Captain K5.*
Captain H.G.D. Stoker. *First Lieutenant K5.*
Commander G.F. Bradshaw. *Captain K15.*
Commander E.R. Dodd. *First Lieutenant K17 and K22.*
Commander L Foley, *Lieutenant K3.*
Commander R. Hennessey.
Commander (E) A.E. Hollamby. *E.R.A. K6 and K26.*
Commander P.J.M. Penney. *Captain K2.*
Commander A.V. Thomas. *Lieutenant K26.*
Captain E.C. Dolling, R.E. (retd.). *Chatham Dockyard, K26.*
Lieutenant-Commander B.D. Youatt. *Sub-Lieutenant K15.*
Dr W. Gover. M.O., *H.M.S. Fearless, leader of 12ᵗʰ Submarine Flotilla, Grand Fleet.*
G.L. Astle. *Signalman K12 and K16.*
A.S. Berry. *Chatham Dockyard K26.*
L.E. Burton. *Chief E.R.A. K26.*
W.L. Campbell. *Beardmore's, builders of K16.*
M.F. Flint.
G.H. Fussell. *E.R.A. K8.*
A.A.V. Gills. *Steward, submarine parent ship H.M.S. Royal Arthur.*
N.H. Guffick. *Lieutenant K9 (former Lieutenant R.N.R.).*

H.M. Homan.
W.E. Howells
D. Logan.
A.F. Miller. *Engineering apprentice, Devonport Dockyard, K6 and K7*
R.H. Mortimer.
F.J.T. Roberts.
J. Scarth. *Stoker K11.*
J.H. Stenhouse.
J.R. Toward. *Acting Chief E.R.A., various K boats.*
J. Watson. *Apprenticed engineer fitter, Fairfield's, builders of K13 and K14.*

Personal MSS.
The Salving of H.M. Submarine K13, by Commander Kenneth Michell.
The War Diary of Oscar Moth. Coxswain K13 and K22.
The Working Drawings of K2, by Commander K.M. Fardell.

The following were lengthy essays or written answers to questions, all of
which involved their authors in much work and call for my special
thanks:
The recollections of Vice-Admiral Sir Robert Ross-Turner. *Captain K8.
Commander 1st Submarine Flotilla, Atlantic Fleet.*
The recollections of Rear-Admiral Allan Poland. *Captain K22 and K26.*
The recollections of Captain Hubert Vaughan Jones. *Captain K6 and K15.*
The recollections of Commander A.H. Ashworth. *First Lieutenant K5.*
The recollections of Commander R.J. Brooke-Booth. *First Lieutenant K3
and K9.*
The recollections of A. Brunton. *E.R.A. K12.*
The recollections of H.T. Cousins. *E.R.A. K2 and K11.*

Interviews
Admiral Sir Geoffrey Layton. *Captain K6.*
Sir William Wallace. *Survivor K13.*
Rear-Admiral E.W. Leir. *Captain K3; Commander 13th Submarine Flotilla,
Grand Fleet.*
The late Captain G. Herbert. *Captain K13.*
Captain R.L. Mackenzie-Edwards. *Lieutenant K22.*
Commander S.M.G. Gravener. *Captain K7 and K16.*
Commander J.C.B. Harbottle. *Captain K14.*
Commander K. Michell. *Captain E50.*
Commander L.C. Rideal. *Survivor K13.*
Commander C. Stevens. *Lieutenant K22.*
Commander J.G. Sutton. *Lieutenant K3.*
J.T. Brett. *E.R.A. submarine parent ships H.M.Ss. Pandora and Royal Arthur.*
H.A. Fulcher. *Stoker 1st class K17.*
W.U. Hancock. *Former Admiralty Electrical Overseer. Survivor K13.*
A. Hime. *Stoker K14.*
J. Lipton. *Draughtsman, Messrs Fairfield.*

APPENDIX B – SOURCES

O. Moth. *Coxswain K13 and K22.*
C. Slade. *E.R.A. K9.*
Mrs A. Riley. *Widow of Signalman Riley, K13.*

Newspapers and Periodicals
The Times.
The Daily Telegraph.
The Daily Express.
The New York Times.
The New York Tribune.
The Naval Review.
The Royal United Services Institute Journal.
The Navy and Military Record.
The Army, Navy and Air Force Gazette.
The Proceedings of the United States Naval Institute.
The Journal of the American Society of Naval Engineers, Inc.
Blackwood's Magazine.
Engineering.
Cornhill Magazine.
The Engineer.
Shipbuilding and Shipping Record.
The Lithgow Journal.
The Navy.
The Journal of the Institute of Naval Architects.
Our Empire Magazine.

Naval and Privately Printed Publications
The Technical History and Index. A serial history of technical problems dealt with by Admiralty departments. (Technical History Section, Admiralty, 1921)
The Naval Staff Monographs, on the 1914–18 war.
British Submarine Organisation, 1914–17.
Two Centuries of Shipbuilding. Scott's Shipbuilding and Engineering Company Ltd., Greenock.
The Accident to Submarine K13, by Percy A. Hillhouse, D.Sc., M.I.N.A. An address to the Greenock Association of Engineers and Shipbuilders, 1919.

Principal Published Works
Fear God and Dread Nought. The correspondence of Admiral of the Fleet Lord Fisher of Kilverstone, edited in three volumes by Arthur J. Marder (Jonathan Cape. 1952–59).
From the Dreadnought to Scapa Flow. Volume One, The Road to War, 1904–14, by Arthur J. Marder (Oxford University Press, 1961).
We Dive at Dawn, by Lieutenant-Commander Kenneth Edwards, R.N. (retd.) (Rich and Cowan, 1939).
Naval Memoirs of Admiral of the Fleet Sir Roger Keyes (Thornton Butterworth,

1934–35).

H.M. Submarines, by Lieutenant-Commander P.K. Kemp, R.N. (Herbert
 Jenkins, 1952).

The British Submarine, by Commander F.W. Lipscomb, O.B.E., R.N. (Black,
 1954).

Jane's Fighting Ships (Sampson Low).

The World Crisis, by Winston Churchill (Thornton Butterworth, 1923–31;
 Odhams Press, 1939).

Libraries, etc.
The following gave me access to their records:

The Lords Commissioners of the Admiralty, who referred me to: *the Chief
 of Naval Information, the Admiralty Library, the Historical Section of the
 Admiralty and the Historical Section of the Flag Officer, Submarines.*
The Librarian of the Imperial War Museum.
The Public Records Office.
The Maida Vale branch of the Paddington Public Library, which holds the
 reserve stock of naval books for the London public libraries.
The Fairfield Shipbuilding and Engineering Company Ltd.

INDEX

A class
A4 27
Aboukir 12, 15
accommodation 70, 115–16
action radius 114–15
Admiralty 15, 64, 109, 118
  *Submarine Administration,
    Training and
    Construction* 76, 107,
    116, 117
  Submarine Development
    Committee 22, 110–11
air intake 113
anti-submarine patrol 71, 73
Archimède 19, 27
armament 17, 22, 28, 66, 73,
  110–11
Armstrong Whitworth, Messrs.
  22, 29, 67, 111
  submarine orders 16, 22, 29,
    109, 111
Ashworth, Lieutenant (*later*
  Commander) A. 117, 120
Asquith, Prime Minister H.H. 14
Atlantic Fleet 117–25
  1st submarine Flotilla 118,
    119, 128, 129, 132
Australia 85, 90, 93, 95, 98, 101

Balfour, First Lord Arthur 110
ballast tank 66, 121, 125, 126,
  129
Barham 85, 92, 101
Bartelott, Captain B. 46–7, 50,
  56
battery flooding 27, 57, 66, 96
battle-cruiser, submersible 117
B.B., Operation 71–3
Beardmore 29, 79, 107
Beatty, Admiral Sir David 20, 21,
  76, 103, 105
  appointment to First Sea
    Lord 117
  Operation B.B. 71, 73
  Operation E.C.1 79–80
Benning, Commander C.S. 73
Black, Sydney 36
Blanche 80

Blonde 73
Boase, Lieutenant-Commander
  B.K. 90–1
boiler-room 21–2, 61, 66–7, 113,
  118
  during diving 29, 69
  fault 26, 32–3, 78, 129
  fire 69
  see also funnel; ventilator
boom defence 86
Bottomley, Horatio 71
Bow Rock 73
Bower, Lieutenant-Commander
  J.G. 78, 93, 98
bows 28, 66
  swan 73, 78, 79, 119
Bradshaw, Commander G.F.,
  D.S.O. 64, 126
bridge 66, 113
bridge-screen 25, 66, 73
Brooke-Booth, Commander R.J.,
  D.S.C., 64
Brown, Leading Seaman F. 96,
  102
Bruce, Lieutenant the
  Honourable John 90
build programme 12
  see also orders
bulkhead 35
Bullen, Frank 36, 40–1, 43, 49–
  50, 52–3, 61

C class 78
  C36 39–40
Calvert, Commander T.F.P. 78,
  93
Canterbury 126
canvas screen 25, 66, 73
carbonic acid 43
censorship 10
Chatham 119, 128
chlorine gas 27, 57, 66, 96
Churchill, Winston 11–12, 13–
  14, 15, 17–18, 20
Cleghorn, Alexander 31, 39, 40
Cocks, Frederick C. 36
Comet 26, 31, 39
compressed air 35–6

conning-tower 25, 28, 29, 44,
  45–6, 66
control-room 61, 123
Cooper, Signalman 97
Corbett, Acting Captain G. 42,
  60
Courageous 80, 85, 86, 87, 92
court martial 10, 105
Court of Inquiry 10
  Battle of May Island 103–5
  K13 accident 60
Cressy 12, 15
crew
  tension in 74
  training 29, 124
Crowther, Commander W. 79,
  106
cruiser submarine 22
Cuddeford, Lieutenant F.W.F.
  120
Curtis, Able Seaman H. 87

D class
  D5 27
Damerell, Stoker Petty Officer
  W. 86, 88
Dardanelles 21, 22
Darke, Lieutenant-Commander
  R. 120, 122–3
Daubin, Lieutenant F.A. 131
Dawson, Sir Trevor 16
de Burgh,
  Lieutenant-Commander C.,
  D.S.O. 74
  K16 trials 107–8
  May Island 78, 85, 89, 91–2,
    104–5
de Burgh, Mrs 74
deafness 63
depth 68
depth-charge thrower 73
design 9, 16, 21–2, 28–9
Devastator 28
Devonport 19, 65
Dickinson, Lieutenant L. 85, 88,
  89
diesel engine 21, 30, 70
dip-chick 112

displacement 28, 131
diver 42, 43
diving 67–70, 107–8, 116, 124
  nose-dive 30, 64, 67, 77, 118
  rudder 69–70, 108, 133
Dobson, Commander 77–8
Dodd, Lieutenant E. 79, 85, 96
Dowding, Stoker 1st Class A. 96, 102
Drake, Able Seaman 96
Dreadnought 134
dreadnought submarine 110, 111
Duncan, Captain J. 36, 37, 41, 43, 59

E class 17, 18, 77–8
  E6 20
  E22 27
  E50 31, 34, 39, 46, 48, 59
E.C.1, Operation 79–106
electrical motor 64–5
Ellerton, Captain W.M. 103
engine 16–17, 21, 30, 70
Engineer, The 129, 130–1
engine-room 22, 61, 67
Evan-Thomas, Sir Hugh 80, 85
Experimental Half-Flotilla 132
explosion 64, 118

F class 18
Fair Isle Channel 72–3
Fairfield Shipbuilding Company 22, 24–5, 41–2, 66
Fearless 77, 85, 99–100, 101–3, 105
  collision with K17 83, 94–8
Fenner, Lieutenant-Commander A. 79, 105
Fessenden 36
Fielder, William 87
Fielman, Commander F.E.B. 60
fire 34, 64–5, 69, 118
Firth of Forth 12, 119
  see also May Island, Battle of
Fisher, Lord "Jacky" 9, 13–14, 18, 20–1, 22, 109
  prewar view on submarines 15
  submarine dreadnought 110, 111
flashback 22, 67
fleet submarine 19–21, 71, 73, 119, 128
  Naval Society address 113–16
  in United States Navy 131–2
Fleming, Staff Surgeon A.F. 99, 102
Foley, Sub-Lieutenant L.F. 30, 98
Formidable 18

France 19, 131
fuel
  feed problem (losing suction) 68, 100, 118, 120
  tank 68, 70
Fulcher, Stoker 1st Class H. 96, 102
funnel 9, 19, 21, 67, 71, 79, 113
  sea down 30, 78, 108–9

G class 18
Gabriel 90
Gaimes, Lieutenant-Commander J.A., D.S.O. 118–19, 120
Gardener, Acting Engineer-Lieutenant T. 104
Gareloch 26, 29–60, 107–8
Geddes, Sir Eric C. 105
generator 67
George V 29, 71
George VI 29–30
German High Seas Fleet 71, 116
German submarine speed 18
Germany 13
Goodenough, Rear-Admiral W.E. 103
Goodhart, Commander F. 37, 38, 44–7, 60, 61, 62
Goodhart, Mrs 43, 50
Gossamer 42, 46
Gracie, Alexander 42, 48
Grand Fleet 11, 71, 114–15, 117
  2nd Battle Cruiser Squadron 80, 85, 90, 94
  1st, 3rd and 4th Light Cruiser Squadrons
  5th Battle Squadron 80, 101
  12th Submarine Flotilla 71, 73, 77–8, 80, 94, 98
    May Island 84, 85
  13th Submarine Flotilla 75, 77, 80, 98
    May Island 85, 86, 90
  see also Operation E.C.1
  see also under K class
Gravener, Lieutenant-Commander S.M.G. 78, 100–1, 102
  assumes command of K7 76–7
Gravener, Mrs 77
Green, John 36, 40–1

H class 18
  H24 128
  H42 128
Hall, Admiral Sir Reginald, M.P. 117
Hall, Commodore S. 21, 28, 60, 105–6, 110–11

on K3 trials 29
as Rear-Admiral 123–4
reservations about K class 22–3
Hammond, Mrs A.I. 64
Hancock, William 34, 36, 41, 43, 49, 54
Harbottle, Commander T.C.B. 77, 87–8, 89–90, 105
Hawke 12
Hawksley, Captain J.R.P. 90–1
Hearn, Commander 78
Heligoland Bight 19, 20
Hepworth, Edward 33, 35, 36, 38
Herbert, Lieutenant-Commander G. 19, 39–40, 40
  K13 disaster 24–9, 30–8, 44–7, 50–4, 56–60, 61, 63
Herbert, Mrs Elizabeth 24, 41–3, 48, 50
Hillhouse, Professor P. 25–6, 37–8, 45, 56, 57, 59
Hills, Stoker 1st Class F.F. 64
Hime, Arthur 66
Hogue 12, 15
Hole, Frederick 37
Holland, John P. 15
Hood, Donald 36
Horton, Admiral Sir Max 113
Hutchings, Commander J. 78, 118
hydroplane 69–70, 108, 133

Inconstant 118, 120–2, 123
Indomitable 85, 90
Inflexible 82, 85, 90–2, 101, 104–5
Italy 16, 131
Ithuriel 77, 85–7, 89, 90, 94, 95, 98, 103
  signalling delay 92–3, 102
  track 82, 83

J class 19, 21
Jackson, Lieutenant G.A. 96, 97, 102, 105
Japan 131
Jellicoe, Admiral Sir John 11, 20, 21
John Brown and Company 31

K class
  K1 64–5, 71, 72–3
  K2 67, 68–9, 74, 77, 125, 129
    Operation B.B. 71, 72
    post-war 119
    trials 30, 64, 65
  K3 29–30, 64, 66, 77, 78, 117

May Island 85, 94, 98, 99, 101, 103
K4 30, 65–6, 71, 73, 78, 79
May Island 85, 94, 98, 99–100, 103–4
K5 78, 118–19, 120, 121, 122–3, 125
K6 30, 65, 70, 71, 76, 77, 129
May Island 85, 94–5, 98–101, 102, 103, 106
swan bows 79
K7 65, 71, 72, 76–7, 78, 117
May Island 85, 94, 100–1, 102, 103
K8 69, 71, 78, 116, 118, 120, 128
K9 68, 78–9, 120–1, 128
K10 64, 77, 119
K11 67, 69, 78, 120
May Island 85, 87, 93–4, 98, 102, 103
K12 78, 116, 129
May Island 85, 87, 90, 93, 98, 101, 103
K13
disaster 24–7, 30–8, 39–63
salvage 59–60, 62
see also K22
K14 25, 60, 62, 66, 77, 118
May Island 82, 85, 87–90, 92, 101–4
K15 79, 107, 108–9, 118, 120, 126–7
K16 79, 107–8, 119
K17 78, 79
May Island 83, 85, 87, 90, 94–7, 101–3, 105
K18 111, 112
K19 111
K20 111, 128
see also M3
K21 111
K22 63, 74–5, 78, 79, 129
Atlantic Fleet exercise 120, 121
May Island 82, 85–6, 88–92, 96, 101, 103, 104–5
see also K13
K26 128, 129, 132
K23–K28 109
rôle 123–4
Kaigun 131
Kay, Lieutenant I. 42, 47
keel 36
Kellett, Lieutenant-Commander G. 72, 76

Kemp, Lieutenant-Commander P.K. 128
Keyes, Commodore R. 13–14, 15–16, 19, 20, 21
Kimbell, Signalman G. 94, 96, 102
Kirk, William 37
K.K. patrol 108–9
Kure 131

L class
L24 128–9
Lake, Robert 36, 43, 49, 61
Lane, Engineer-Lieutenant A. 26, 31–3, 35, 37, 60, 62
Largo Bay 119
Laurence, Commander N. 65, 77
Layard, Commander 78
layout 28–9
Layton, Commander G. 28–9
May Island 70, 77, 79, 94–5, 99, 100, 102, 105–6
Swordfish 22
Lees, Captain E. 13
Leir, Commander E.W. 29–30, 77, 85, 90, 92–3
as Rear-Admiral 76
length 28, 67
Leveson, Rear-Admiral A.C. 90, 93, 95
Lewis, William 37
Lipton, John 52
Little, Captain C.J.C. 77, 85, 94, 95–6, 102, 103, 105
Lloyds 130
London Navy Treaty 1930 131
losing suction 68, 100, 118, 120
Lowestoft 20

M class (mutton boat) 111–12, 117, 128
M1 111, 112, 128, 130
M2 128, 132–3
M3 111, 128, 132, 133
MacIntyre, Annie 34, 62
MacKinnon, Percy 130–1
Macmillan, Hugh 25–6, 31, 39
Mark-Wardlaw, Alexander 65
May Island, Battle of 76–106
diagrammatic layout of fleet 80–4
naval security 112–13
McLean, William 36, 43, 48, 49–50, 52–3, 58, 61
Michell, Lieutenant-Commander K. 31, 34
raises alarm 39–40
rescue of K13 43, 46–8, 50–2, 53, 54–6, 59, 61
monitor submarine 111

Moth, Chief Petty Officer O. 54, 57–9, 63, 74, 105
K13 disaster 33, 36, 37, 38
May Island 85–6, 88, 91, 92
opinion on K boats 104, 133
Mountbatten, Lord Louis F.A.V.N. 76

Naismith, Lieutenant M. 27
Nautilus 17, 134
naval
dockyard 19, 22, 64–5
policy 132
Naval Intelligence Division 13
Naval Review 14, 119
Naval Society address 113–16
Neate, Frank 37
New Zealand 85
Newhaven Packet 74
nose-dive 30, 64, 67, 77, 118
Nova Scotia 92
nuclear submarine 134–5

Observer 72
Ocean type 17
oil, freezing 65, 66
Operation B.B. 71–3
Operation E.C.1 79–106
orders 9, 16, 18, 22, 29, 109, 112
Orion 103
Oversea design 16–18

Pathfinder 12
patrol 71, 73, 108–9, 115
Pembroke naval dockyard 19
Pentland Firth 67, 109
periscope 28
Poland, Commander A. 121–2
Portland Harbour 129
Portsmouth naval dockyard 19, 22, 64–5
"pothole" 109
power unit 21
Powney, Edward 37
pressure 35, 68
hull 123, 129

Q ship 27
Queen Elizabeth 80

Renfrew, Donald 36
Resolution 128–9
Rideal, Lieutenant (E) L. 32, 33, 36, 63
Rigby, Temporary Lieutenant R. 86
Riley, Leading Signalman A. 49, 50, 63
Rocket 72
roll over 22

Ross-Turner,
  Lieutenant-Commander R.
  29, 78
Rosyth 75, 76
Royal Navy
  see Admiralty; Grand Fleet

S class 18
salvage 126
Sandford, Lieutenant R.D. 95,
  98–9, 102
Scapa Flow 11, 68–9
Scott, Admiral Sir Percy 15, 134
Scotts, Messrs., of Greenock 16–
  17, 29, 79, 107
sea, heavy 66, 67, 78, 113
Searle, Frederick 26, 36, 49, 50,
  61
seaworthiness 66–7, 73, 78, 108,
  113, 116, 119, 124
Selley, L. 65
Shandon Hydropathic Hotel 26,
  34, 74, 108
Shieldhall 25
Shove, Lieutenant-Commander
  H.W. 78, 98, 109
Singer, Lieutenant P.G. 25, 32,
  33, 36, 45, 49, 59–61, 63
size 28, 109–10
Skinner, Edward 36, 41, 43, 54,
  61
Smith, William 37
Sonnava 25
Southampton 78–9
speed 9, 107, 113, 116
  surface 17, 18, 21
  trial 30
Start Point 130
Steel, John 37, 62
steering gear 104
  failure 25, 87–8, 107

stern 70
  light 85
Stewart, Stoker Petty Officer J.
  96, 102
Stocks, Commander D. 73, 78,
  98
stoker 66–7
Strachan, William 37
strategy 14–15, 20
Struthers, William 32, 33–4, 35,
  36, 40–1
submarine
  campaign against 130–1
  numbers at start of war 13
  rôle of 19–20, 123–4
Submarine Service 12, 13, 129
submerged endurance 116
superstructure 28, 67, 113, 115
Surcouf 131
Swan and Hunter 79
Swift 20
Swordfish 16–17, 22, 77

tactics 14–15, 119
telephone buoy 40
Tennyson-d'Eyncourt, Sir
  Eustace 18–19
  submarine design 17, 21, 22,
  24
Thompson, Commander G.P.
  132
Thrush 42, 47, 51, 55, 59
Tillard, Commander A.T. 60
Tor Bay 119, 120
torpedo 110–11
  human 28
torpedo tube 22, 114
torpedo-room 35, 40, 41, 57
trials 29–30, 64–7, 74–5, 107–8
  see also K13 disaster
trimming 67–8, 68–9, 124

U-boat 12, 13, 18, 71–3
  U9 12, 15
  U27 27
  U95 72
  U139 type 116
underwater performance 69–70
U.S. Navy 131–2, 134

V class 18
Vancouver, H.M.S. 128
Vass, Stoker 1st Class K. 97, 102
Vaughan Jones,
  Lieutenant-Commander H.
  79, 85, 91, 107
  on K15 108–9, 126–7
Venetia 101, 103
ventilation 70
ventilator 21, 26, 51–2, 60, 65,
  66–7, 121
Versatile 128
Vickers, Sons and Maxim 15,
  16–17, 66, 111, 128
  submarine orders 21, 22, 29,
  109
Victory Cruise 117
Vidar 130
voice pipe 34

W class 18
Wallace, William 36, 41, 48, 49,
  59, 62–3
War Emergency Programme 18
weather 66, 67, 78, 113
Westbrook, Leading Seaman A.
  96, 97, 102
wheelhouse 29, 74
wireless mast 28, 41

Young, Captain F. 43, 48, 56, 60,
  62